PRIDE AND PREJUDICE

by Jane Austen

Adapted by Sara Pascoe

SAMUEL FRENCH

samuelfrench.co.uk

FOR AMATEUR PRODUCTION ENQUIRIES

UNITED KINGDOM AND WORLD
EXCLUDING NORTH AMERICA
plays@samuelfrench.co.uk
020 7255 4302/01

Each title is subject to availability from Samuel French,
depending upon country of performance.

Cover image designer © Gemma Leggett

Photographer: Alan Fletcher www.ashotinthedark.com

Acting Editions

BORN TO PERFORM

Playscripts designed from the ground up to work the way you do in rehearsal, performance and study

---

Larger, clearer text for easier reading

Wider margins for notes

Performance features such as character and props lists, sound and lighting cues, and more

---

+ CHOOSE A SIZE AND STYLE TO SUIT YOU

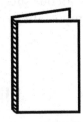

STANDARD EDITION

Our regular paperback book at our regular size

SPIRAL-BOUND EDITION

The same size as the Standard Edition, but with a sturdy, easy-to-fold, easy-to-hold spiral-bound spine

LARGE EDITION

A4 size and spiral bound, with larger text and a blank page for notes opposite every page of text. Perfect for technical and directing use

LEARN MORE | **samuelfrench.co.uk/actingeditions**

FIND PERFECT PLAYS TO PERFORM AT
www.samuelfrench.co.uk/perform

MUSIC USE NOTE

Licensees are solely responsible for obtaining formal written permission from copyright owners to use copyrighted music in the performance of this play and are strongly cautioned to do so. If no such permission is obtained by the licensee, then the licensee must use only original music that the licensee owns and controls. Licensees are solely responsible and liable for all music clearances and shall indemnify the copyright owners of the play(s) and their licensing agent, Samuel French, against any costs, expenses, losses and liabilities arising from the use of music by licensees. Please contact the appropriate music licensing authority in your territory for the rights to any incidental music.

See page 122 for further information.

IMPORTANT BILLING AND CREDIT REQUIREMENTS

If you have obtained performance rights to this title, please refer to your licensing agreement for important billing and credit requirements. A licence issued by Samuel French Ltd to perform this play does not include permission to use the incidental music specified in this copy.

Where the place of performance is already licensed by the PERFORMING RIGHT SOCIETY (PRS) a return of the music used must be made to them. If the place of performance is not so licensed then application should be made to the PRS, 2 Pancras Square, London, N1C 4AG.

A separate and additional licence from PHONOGRAPHIC PERFORMANCE LTD, 1 Upper James Street, London W1F 9DE (www.ppluk.com) is needed whenever commercial recordings are used.

ABOUT THE AUTHOR

SARA PASCOE is an actress, writer and one of the most accomplished comedians in the country.

A multi-award-winning stand up, Sara has filmed her own comedy special: *Sara Pascoe Live from the BBC* and both guest starred on and hosted episodes of *Live at the Apollo* (BBC). Sara starred throughout the second series of *Taskmaster* (Dave) and is a regular guest on *Frankie Boyle's New World Order* and on shows such as *QI* and *Have I Got News For You?* (BBC).

As an actress, Sara has an impressive array of TV credits including the BAFTA nominated *Twenty Twelve* (BBC2), *W1A* (BBC2), *Campus* (C4), *The Thick of It* (BBC2) and *Being Human* (BBC3).

Sara's debut book *Animal* was published in May 2016 (Faber & Faber) to widespread critical acclaim. Sara's second book *Sex Power Money* (Faber & Faber) and radio series *Modern Monkey* (BBC Radio 4) are due for release in 2018.

Pride and Prejudice, adapted by Sara Pascoe, based on the novel by Jane Austen, commissioned by Nottingham Playhouse, was first performed in a co-production between Nottingham Playhouse Theatre Company and York Theatre Royal, at Nottingham Playhouse on 15th September 2017 with the following cast and creative team:

ELIZABETH / TEACHER ELIZABETH	Bethan Mary-James
JANE / MODERN JANE	Rebecca D'Souza
MARY / MODERN MARY /	
MISS DE BOURGH / MRS HURST	Rachel Partington
KITTY / MODERN KITTY / CHARLOTTE LUCAS /	
MODERN CHARLOTTE / MISS DARCY	Alice Haig
LYDIA / MODERN LYDIA / MISS BINGLEY /	
MRS GARDINER	Olivia Onyehara
MRS BENNET / MODERN MRS BENNET /	
LADY CATHERINE DE BOURGH / HOUSEKEEPER	Kerry Peers
MR DARCY	Matt Whitchurch
MR BINGLEY / MR COLLINS	Matthew Romain
MR WICKHAM / MODERN WICKHAM /	
MR GARDINER	Alex Sawyer
MR BENNET / GRAHAM	Adrian Irvine

Director	Susannah Tresilian
Designer	Carla Goodman
Lighting Designer	Mark Howland
Music By	Emmy The Great
Sound Designer	Drew Baumohl
Video Designer	Andrew Bullett
Movement Director	Adele Parry
Assistant Director	Justine Sharp

SCENE BREAKDOWN

ACKNOWLEDGEMENTS

I am grateful to a world of women, especially my younger sisters who married before me and my mother who preached independence above all. I thank Katie and Vanessa for being the funniest and most curious humans, Susannah and Emmy for creating this opportunity and extending my every understanding of what we were making. I thank Dawn Sedgwick that I never need wait for a man with property.

I'm so grateful to have been born to a society that's freed its women enough that we may change it more.

Love to all the maids. X

For my sister, Cheryl Elizabeth.

CHARACTER LIST / ROLE BREAKDOWN

ELIZABETH
TEACHER ELIZABETH
DARCY
JANE
MODERN JANE
MR BINGLEY
MR COLLINS
MR BENNET
GRAHAM
MRS BENNET
MODERN MRS BENNET
LADY CATHERINE
HOUSEKEEPER KITTY
MODERN KITTY
CHARLOTTE LUCAS
MODERN CHARLOTTE
MISS DARCY
LYDIA
MODERN LYDIA
MISS BINGLEY
MRS GARDINER
MARY
MODERN MARY
MRS HURST
MISS DE BOURGH
MR WICKHAM
MODERN WICKHAM
MR GARDINER

ACT ONE

Scene One: Home

Piano music plays and a woman's weak, reedy voice sings as a drawing room builds around her. The song is a tragedy, about a sad old woman who is unmarried in her thirties. Sung by LYDIA *who is confident and inept.* KITTY *stands next to her at the piano,* MARY *reads a book on a sofa,* ELIZABETH *and* JANE *are playing chess and whispering.* MR BENNET *reads a newspaper at the table.*

Sound effects door slam. A crash.

MRS BENNET *(offstage) Yes!*

MRS BENNET *enters. She whispers loudly enough for the whole world to hear.*

(whisper) He has taken it.

MR BENNET Has he? Who?

MRS BENNET *(whisper)* Bingley.

MR BENNET What was it?

MRS BENNET *(too annoyed to whisper)* Netherfield Park.

MR BENNET *(joking)* And to *where* has he—

MRS BENNET *(ignoring him)* Unmarried. Large fortune. Twenty servants, four horses, *that we know of...*

MR BENNET What's his name?

MRS BENNET Four or five thousand a year Mrs Long says.

LYDIA Five thousand?

JANE Is he handsome?

LYDIA When shall we see him?

MRS BENNET Girls girls, be calm and sensible. You know your
father must go first.

KITTY When will that be?

LYDIA And then the rest of us?

ELIZABETH Remember, Jane first.

JANE Me first.

ELIZABETH *(to* LYDIA*)* She has most to recommend her.

LYDIA But then me.

MRS BENNET *(to* MR BENNET*)* Then Lydia truly.

KITTY When will he go?

MR BENNET He?

ELIZABETH Perhaps Jane should go with him.

MRS BENNET Hush Lizzy, that just isn't done.

MR BENNET I'll send Lizzy with a letter. Easy.

ELIZABETH/MRS BENNET Daddy?/Not Elizabeth!

ELIZABETH Why not me?

MRS BENNET Why must you vex me Mr Bennet?

MARY What *colour* were the horses?

MRS BENNET My poor nerves.

MR BENNET My poor ears listening to your poor nerves.

JANE Perhaps Mrs Long can introduce us?

MRS BENNET *(to* JANE*)* She has those nieces, she is—

LYDIA Of course.

MRS BENNET Selfish!

KITTY Blasted nieces!

MRS BENNET (*sweetly to* **MR B**) You will visit my dear?

MR BENNET I won't.

MRS BENNET FOUR THOUSAND!

LYDIA Or five!

MRS BENNET I'm sick! My nerves! You tear me to pieces.

MR BENNET I will not go, as I need not attend the man.

MRS BENNET Put your daughters' needs before your own – what? What is it? Pride? Laziness?

MR BENNET If you would just give me a second—

LYDIA Why should we give you *anything* Daddy?

KITTY When you do nothing for us?

ELIZABETH It would help if you just—

MR BENNET I'm trying to explain—

ELIZABETH Not for me, but for Jane.

JANE I would only marry for a *very* great love!

LYDIA (*to* **JANE**) Five. Thousand.

MR BENNET I won't go over to introduce myself...

LYDIA/MRS BENNET/KITTY/JANE Weasel!/Monster!/Pig!/My heart is broken!

MR BENNET ...that would be silly...

MRS BENNET JUDAS!

MR BENNET ...for I have already been.

Beat. Then a wave of sweetness.

LYDIA Dotty old bear...

ELIZABETH Well done daddy.

ELIZABETH *kisses her father and exits.*

JANE You really are wonderful.

LYDIA We may go?

MRS BENNET Why on earth didn't you say?

MR BENNET Where's the fun?

MRS BENNET What an excellent father you have.

MR BENNET I rather liked Mr Bingley.

MARY And the horses?

MR BENNET We met by accident as he explored the land. Very polite and interested he seemed.

JANE Did he ask about us?

LYDIA Is he taller than me?

JANE Will he expect our call?

KITTY Does he know the soldiers?

MRS BENNET Now everybody come on, time for calm. Sit down.

MRS BENNET sits for a split second before jumping up again.

Bring me your best dresses and we'll see what needs doing!

Lights dim. The sound of chalk on a blackboard. Lights up on a section of the stage while the ball scene is created around them. A TEACHER is writing fluidly, the sentence becomes legible seconds later. She reads it aloud.

TEACHER ELIZABETH "It is a truth universally acknowledged that a single man in possession of a good fortune must be in want of a wife."

ELIZABETH underlines the words truth, man and wife. She turns to the audience and as if addressing a class of children.

Can anybody tell me what "heteronormative" means?

Blackboard swings away, **TEACHER ELIZABETH** *becomes* **ELIZABETH** *with the removal or addition of wig/costume or another physical signifier. This continues with the doubling throughout the play – sometimes changes are very quick so best to keep details small and differentiate with performance.*

Scene Two: Village Ball

The girls fetch fabric and hats, this becomes a form of dance, some of them can be holding tailcoats or top hats as partners. More people enter until the stage is full and the drawing room dismantled. Music will signify time passing throughout the scene, speeding up in between dialogue. MRS BENNET *is talking to an older woman (she could be a mannequin or made from props).*

MRS BENNET A party of twenty! Well that excuses his being away all this time, SIXTEEN LADIES? Why would he bring all those women when I...when there is, I mean when there are so *many* girls here. Unmarried young girls. It's, I mean he's greedy I should—

MRS BENNET *rushes off.* LYDIA, KITTY, MARY, JANE *and* ELIZABETH *awkwardly waiting at side of dance.*

LYDIA Even though I am the youngest, I am still the tallest and so perhaps he will ask me to dance first.

ELIZABETH That wouldn't be fair Lydia.

KITTY *(to* LYDIA*)* We shouldn't stand with Lizzy and Jane just in case—

JANE I am not going to cry Kitty!

ELIZABETH Which one is he?

LYDIA We were supposed to meet him *before* tonight, not hanging about like this.

KITTY We could be anyone, any stranger, rather than the man's closest and most special neighbours.

LYDIA I'm going to move nearer.

KITTY *I'm* going to move nearer.

LYDIA *and* KITTY *pathetically attempt to get in the eyeline of* BINGLEY.

ELIZABETH It is a crushing shame that the man has been away to London all this time.

JANE But he had to go gather his party.

ELIZABETH Pardon me Jane, I wasn't criticising, I... So what do you think?

MARY It's like nobody even realises there's a war on.

JANE He seems very smiley.

MARY Exactly.

ELIZABETH And of good height.

> **MRS BENNET** *pushes in-between* **JANE** *and* **LIZZY**.

MRS BENNET Mrs Long said he'd brought twenty, sixteen of whom were young women.

ELIZABETH SIXTEEN!

JANE Who are they?

MRS BENNET BUT Mrs Lucas said he arrived yesterday with only ten, and over half of the Ladies were Gentlemen...

JANE Still...

MRS BENNET Wait – there is news of a richer man! A Mr Darcy! Twenty thousand a year!

> **MRS BENNET** *gestures at* **MR DARCY**, **LYDIA** *is currently trying to get his attention.*

ELIZABETH He's even taller!

JANE Mama, who are the women?

MRS BENNET And that's the thing, all five are sisters!

JANE Thank G— I mean, how wonderful to be five sisters. And for us to have so many new acquaintances to make.

> *They hush as* **BINGLEY** *and* **CHARLOTTE** *dance over. They watch as they thank each other. Music changes.*

CHARLOTTE *seems demure and sweet as she approaches the group. She checks over her shoulder that* BINGLEY *has gone before speaking excitedly.*

CHARLOTTE Two sisters, not five. One of them married. It's just the four of them at Netherfield.

MRS BENNET You heard about Mr Darcy?

CHARLOTTE Twenty grand a year!

CHARLOTTE *and* MRS BENNET *both laugh.* CHARLOTTE *hugs* JANE *and* ELIZABETH.

How are my favourite neighbours?

The music stops for a moment and MARY *speaks very loudly:*

MARY Daddy's got gout.

BINGLEY *comes over and asks* JANE *to dance. A new song plays.* ELIZABETH, MARY *and* CHARLOTTE *take up their partners. As they dance away,* MR BENNET *approaches limping and merry.* MR DARCY *slouches nearby noticeably listening.*

MR BENNET 'Twas a night like this.

MRS BENNET What?

MR BENNET Twinkle at me my Wife, twinkle at me, give me a wink.

MRS BENNET You're going to snore later.

MR BENNET They're in place now. All the young people mixing like butterflies. Leave them to it I'd say.

MRS BENNET If he would just take one, at least one.

MR BENNET You've done everything you can.

MRS BENNET But he must. If we get a match for Jane, or Lydia, and she'll be so nearby.

MR BENNET You're perspiring my dear.

MRS BENNET All that money, and the house...

MR BENNET I know, but let us enjoy an evening?

MRS BENNET And once one is matched, she can help with her sisters, and once they are all matched, I can relax. And only then—

MR BENNET Perhaps we—

MRS BENNET ...can I die. Quietly. My work being done.

MR DARCY looks appalled and moves away. Song changes. ELIZABETH *sits down.* MR BENNET *pulls* MRS BENNET *to him and they dance closely.*

MR BENNET I'm sorry.

MRS BENNET It's not your fault.

MR BENNET If only we'd been blessed with a boy.

MRS BENNET Or the early one, if he'd lived.

They think and dance.

MR BENNET 'Twas a night like this...

MRS BENNET What?

MR BENNET When I first saw you puppy. I'm reminded of it, the awkwardness and polite smiles and clumsy dancing – and then, in lilac my—

MRS BENNET Plum. It was plum.

MR BENNET ...love. So shy seeming, yet your eyes met mine and never left.

MR BENNET stops to look at MRS BENNET, *he touches her face. She looks back at him.*

MRS BENNET It was nothing like this. The people that night were of much poorer quality.

Song changes. Couples move around the stage.

WHY IS ELIZABETH NOT DANCING?

ELIZABETH *sits reading a book, a couple of feet from* **MR BINGLEY** *and* **MR DARCY**.

MR DARCY Can we leave now?

MR BINGLEY *roars with laughter,* **ELIZABETH** *looks over at them.*

Surely you've danced with them all.

MR BINGLEY Some more than once, while you've danced with—

MR DARCY I hate dancing.

MR BINGLEY ...my sisters.

MR DARCY I don't know anybody else here.

MR BINGLEY Get to know them, by dancing and talking and—

MR DARCY Pardon me, I misspoke. I do not *wish* to know anybody here.

MR BINGLEY Some of the girls are—

MR DARCY Money grabbing?

MR BINGLEY ...beautiful.

MR DARCY You were dancing with the only decent one.

MR BINGLEY Miss Bennet. She's absolutely—

MR DARCY She smiles too much.

MR BINGLEY ...*lovely*. Ever so sweet that one, and she's clever and—

MR DARCY She'll do for country.

MR BINGLEY Don't look, she has a sister – just behind us, you could ask her.

MR DARCY *looks.*

She's not *quite* as pretty as her sister.

MR DARCY I'm sure she'll make some pig farmer very happy.

MR BINGLEY Sorry Mr Metropolitan.

MR DARCY She'll not need a spade with those arms.

MR BINGLEY You're worse than usual this evening.

MR DARCY These wedding-hungry hill-dwellers have put my back up. Let's—

MR DARCY/MR BINGLEY ...go/dance!

Music changes, MR BINGLEY *goes back to* JANE *for second dance,* MR DARCY *is approached by* MISS BINGLEY.

MISS BINGLEY My sister dances with her husband.

MR DARCY The scandal.

MISS BINGLEY You'll keep me company?

MR DARCY Much obliged.

A couple of feet away MRS BENNET *rushes over to* ELIZABETH *and snatches the book from her hands.*

MRS BENNET Get up and dance this instant.

ELIZABETH I can't force a man to ask me.

MRS BENNET *(gesturing to* MR DARCY*)* Him.

ELIZABETH I'd rather sit out the rest of the night! The rest of my life!

MRS BENNET Stubborn creature.

ELIZABETH *(whisper)* I don't care Mama, and you mustn't, but the gentleman referred to me as an—

MR DARCY ...Aberdeen Angus.

MISS BINGLEY You're ever so silly that's a male.

MR DARCY They should not have put a dress on him.

MISS BINGLEY *(laughing)* And what about her?

MR DARCY Another Friesian.

MISS BINGLEY You're wasted in drawing rooms.

MR DARCY Indeed.

MISS BINGLEY You belong in the menagerie.

MR DARCY I wish your brother would hurry up and—

MISS BINGLEY Dance his legs off? Find a wife?

MR DARCY Heaven forefend! Not here.

MISS BINGLEY Do you take this – Shire horse to be your lawful wedded—

Focus returns to **ELIZABETH** *and* **MRS BENNET**.

MRS BENNET ...windy wallets over there, ruining the ball for everyone. Why come then?

ELIZABETH We're lucky it is not *he* set to be our neighbour.

MRS BENNET Behaving like they're better than us when it is widely known their fortune comes from industry.

ELIZABETH I'll not tarnish Mr Bingley with his associations, at least I'll try.

MRS BENNET He cannot take his eyes from Jane's!

ELIZABETH How can one friend be so warm and kindly and the other...? NO, that's enough. I'll not think of him any longer.

MRS BENNET Let us tear Jane away, let Mr Bingley feel the drabness of a ball without the most beautiful woman.

ELIZABETH You're very good at this mother.

ELIZABETH *gets up to walk over to* **JANE**.

MR DARCY I can't bear this meat market a second longer.

MISS BINGLEY Tell my brother I am faint. He cannot deny us then.

MR DARCY *walks over to* **MR BINGLEY.** *Music becomes slow and romantic as* **ELIZABETH** *and* **MR DARCY** *arrive next to* **JANE** *and* **MR BINGLEY,** *who separate but are still staring at each other.* **MR DARCY** *and* **ELIZABETH** *are posed perfectly for as if they were about to dance. Their eyes meet. They each look furious. A beat.* **JANE** *and* **MR BINGLEY** *notice and turn.*

MR DARCY Goodnight, Miss...?

ELIZABETH Goodbye.

Blackout, loud music, lights up.

Scene Three: School

TEACHER ELIZABETH *in front of a blackboard with scribbles relating to characters and social class on it. STUDENT KITTY and STUDENT LYDIA are wearing corsets on top of school uniform.*

TEACHER ELIZABETH ...at this point, you could call it a "will they/won't they?"

STUDENT LYDIA Hopefully they won't.

TEACHER ELIZABETH That's why it's such a clever story, and this is like, a hundred years before Ross and Rachel.

STUDENT LYDIA Who?

STUDENT KITTY He's really horrible Miss, but is that supposed to be okay because her parents are money grabbing?

TEACHER ELIZABETH Her parents are, *aware* of money let's say. They are conscious, but only because if their daughters don't get married... Well, you'll see.

STUDENT LYDIA Everyone in the book is awful.

TEACHER ELIZABETH Perhaps we are going to find out why?

STUDENT LYDIA 'Cause it's the olden days?

STUDENT KITTY They shouldn't care about weddings, they should DO something.

STUDENT LYDIA Not sitting around knitting and whatever.

TEACHER ELIZABETH If you can read from the top of page twenty-nine... Jane...

Enter JANE *reading from a piece of paper, the scene changes around her, a new drawing room is created.*

JANE *(reading a letter)* ...if you are disposed to visiting us here at Netherfield?

JANE *waves the paper.*

(shouting) Everyone! We've been invited to visit our neighbours!

JANE *turns her eyes back to the letter.*

(reading) We would love to get to know you better so please come *all by yourself so* that we might share the secrets of our bosoms and become the greatest friends.

MARY *pops her head in.*

MARY Teatime?

JANE I'm ever so sorry Mary, they want me to go alone.

MARY I've eaten all the crusts from the bird table!

MARY *exits.*

JANE How exquisite, I am to make new friends!

JANE *spins from the stage.* CHARLOTTE *and* ELIZABETH *walk arm in arm.*

Scene Four: Lizzy And Charlotte Walk

CHARLOTTE It is so inspiring to have such well-bred women in the district, you are so lucky Miss Bingley and Mrs Hurst have taken a liking to the two of you.

ELIZABETH Charlotte, they barely tolerate me. It is Jane they love.

CHARLOTTE You must find out where they get their dresses made.

ELIZABETH I'm loathe to give them such compliments as they eat them up and then condescend so smugly – I am never allowed to forget *their* awareness of *my* inferiority.

CHARLOTTE Do not be proud Lizzy, these ladies might soon be your relations – how is the...?

ELIZABETH There is no match. Mr Bingley shows my sister attention at dinners, they have long and frivolous conversations but that is—

CHARLOTTE She must get him alone.

ELIZABETH Remember this is our modest Jane, she is inscrutable, giving away nothing.

CHARLOTTE She is silly, if Mr Bingley had shown any interest in myself...other than being the first he asked to dance.

CHARLOTTE *waits.*

ELIZABETH Congratulations again.

CHARLOTTE He must have thought me striking to have asked me before any other?

ELIZABETH He is incredibly polite.

CHARLOTTE Absolutely dashing.

ELIZABETH Perhaps you were nearest?

CHARLOTTE I may be no beauty Lizzy, but I have plenty to recommend myself...

ELIZABETH I am teasing. I am simply tired of discussing that silly ball, and who danced with whom and when he will propose to my sister.

CHARLOTTE What *I* should have done in Jane's position—

ELIZABETH Turned up to tea with your dowry?

CHARLOTTE You know I have none.

ELIZABETH I'm teasing, continue then?

CHARLOTTE If Mr Bingley had chosen myself for a second dance, I should have said "no".

CHARLOTTE *separates herself from* ELIZABETH *and performs this for her.*

(theatrically) If we were to partner a second time, you would be showing myself favour above all other ladies present, why, our society would begin the most inappropriate chatter about our intentions...

(deeper voice) Whatever do you mean?

Of course, I know you to be a noble and cheerful creature, but ladies of the neighbourhood may suspect your designs upon my hand.

(deeper voice) And what if I do wish to ask for—

ELIZABETH From a second dance? You're doing his proposing for him!

CHARLOTTE It is never too soon to fix them. Let a gentleman know that every action is witnessed and noted and that there are expectations attached.

ELIZABETH There are no expectations with Jane, she has not admitted that she has any feelings or hopes in his direction, and while she colours madly every time my sisters say his name, in his company she talks and laughs with complete freedom from propriety.

CHARLOTTE This is no good...

ELIZABETH She is happy. It is very good.

CHARLOTTE Secure him first. Plenty of time to be happy afterwards. How many dinners?

ELIZABETH Four. During which Mr Bingley only has eyes for her.

CHARLOTTE I hope she will not be humiliated.

ELIZABETH He is too decent, unlike that awf—

CHARLOTTE ...as *I* was after that first dance at the ball. And Mother was chatting away insisting "he'll come back round" but—

ELIZABETH Well done you on being chosen first.

CHARLOTTE I shall always have that I suppose. And the friend! I should have liked to dance with Mr Darcy and created some frictious jealousy!

ELIZABETH Fate has saved you a most unpleasant interaction.

CHARLOTTE Does Darcy remain at Netherfield?

ELIZABETH Much to my chagrin. His game has changed from ignoring me completely, treating my entrance as if I have something stinking stuck on my boot, to now staring at me seriously. He eavesdrops on my conversations, always lingering behind me as if to whisper something horrid in my ear.

CHARLOTTE Perhaps he likes you?

ELIZABETH He does not bother to disguise his finding me provincial and uncultured. I have such fun appalling him. The more he starts at my opinions the more I wish to shock. Just last week I told him I wished I were French and found Napoleon very sensible!

CHARLOTTE You must stop this childishness. You might ruin things for your sister.

ELIZABETH My friend this is *no* existence – tiptoeing around hoping for marriage – we cannot live our lives this way.

CHARLOTTE Without marriage, you will have nowhere to live your lives.

ELIZABETH Says the woman without a dowry...

CHARLOTTE Touché.

ELIZABETH *(laughs)* French! Have I ever told you how much I *admire* Napoleon?

Scene Five: Netherfield

Musical interlude becomes MISS BINGLEY *playing on the piano at Netherfield. Sound effects heavy rain.* MRS HURST *sits and darns.* MR DARCY *stares from a window.*

MISS BINGLEY Ahem. You are supposed to be admiring my playing.

MR DARCY Please assume I am consistently impressed and continue with my compliments assumed.

MISS BINGLEY What purpose a woman's ability if not to gain the applause and attention of her gentleman friends?

MR DARCY You are goading, I will not bite.

MISS BINGLEY Perhaps you will dance when Miss Bennet arrives?

MR DARCY *stares at* MISS BINGLEY.

MR DARCY Keen to get under my hat today?

MISS BINGLEY I know what you were thinking. At the window.

MR DARCY Oh yes?

MISS BINGLEY You were wondering how long we must endure this rainy, awful place—

MR DARCY Incorrect.

MISS BINGLEY ...and these miserable, quite shameless people!

MR DARCY They are, most of them. It is the mother I cannot bear. But she was nowhere in my thoughts...

MISS BINGLEY What concerns you then?

MR DARCY Eyes.

MR DARCY *looks out of the window again.*

There is something that happens to one, in the stomach, when a fine pair of eyes are raised...

MISS BINGLEY *gets up from the piano and walks over to* MR DARCY. *She stands next to him and raises her head slowly.*

...to meet your own. A light within their darkness, a flash of comprehension between beings, a flash of seeing—

MR DARCY *glances down towards* MISS BINGLEY *now who is staring at him with all her power.*

—and being seen. That moment, those eyes. How can I not have noticed before?

Beat as MISS BINGLEY *and* MR DARCY *look at each other.*

Do you not agree that Elizabeth Bennet has very fine eyes?

MISS BINGLEY Good luck with your mother-in-law.

MR DARCY Please congratulate your female mind on its most astonishing leap.

MRS HURST *(shouting)* Hearty congratulations on your nuptials!

MR DARCY I... This is just thoughts and I merely... Excuse me, I do not have to explain myself.

Sound effects bell rings.

MISS BINGLEY Shall I be bridesmaid?

MRS HURST Shall I lend you a leash and whip for her training?

MISS BINGLEY *and* MRS HURST *laugh.* JANE *enters, absolutely soaking.*

JANE I'm ever, ever so sorry about your carpets.

Blackout. Storm sound effects leading to birdsong sound effects.

Scene Six: Breakfast At Longbourn

Lights up, breakfast table in spotlight, rest of stage set as Netherfield drawing room and dark. MRS *and* MR BENNET, ELIZABETH *and* MARY *sit.*

MR BENNET Shall I go and slipper those slug-a-beds?

MRS BENNET No let us begin, we'll eat.

MR BENNET Not until we're all seated, we're not savages.

MRS BENNET *shoves a full piece of bread in her mouth.*

MRS BENNET *(chewing)* They've already gone.

MARY Can I go? Where?

MR BENNET You'd better not be saying what I think you're saying.

MARY Oh no.

ELIZABETH Where have they gone?

MARY Who?

MRS BENNET Let us enjoy a nice breakfast. Cheese?

MR BENNET They'll drown. Or worse!

MRS BENNET Their aunt is with them.

MR BENNET Well unless she has the antidote for absolute silliness I don't know what use she'll be.

ELIZABETH Where are Kitty and Lydia?

MARY I'm feeling very chatty this morning.

MRS BENNET They're at the seaside. That's all. A seaside visit with their aunt and uncle.

MR BENNET They're chasing soldiers.

MRS BENNET Having a little fun.

MR BENNET Why should they have fun when I'm having such a TERRIBLE LIFE?

MRS BENNET We could do a lot worse than a proposal from a captain.

ELIZABETH They're babies.

MRS BENNET I've no patience for age and order when I've so many of you to see secure. And if some of you just sit there like dumplings at balls—

ELIZABETH This is my fault now?!

MRS BENNET *(to* MARY*)* ...and some of you so busy with your head in books you don't realise if your skirts are on back to front.

MARY Poor Lizzy.

MR BENNET I was asked for my permission, I refused it, and you have sneaked behind my back.

MRS BENNET It's only a day by the sea.

Sound effects doorbell. MRS BENNET *jumps up.*

Ooh. That will be news from Netherfield. What a gift that rain!

MR BENNET What is the point of servants if you—

A SERVANT *enters with a letter which he takes over towards* ELIZABETH. MRS BENNET *tries to grab it.* ELIZABETH *stands and walks as she reads.*

MRS BENNET Is this it? Has he proposed?

MARY Can I keep the envelope?

ELIZABETH My poor sister.

MRS BENNET He hasn't then?

ELIZABETH She is sick. From the storm. She's being brave but I can tell she's ever so—

MRS BENNET She's staying there? Clever girl Jane!

MR BENNET Your eldest daughter flattened in pursuit of a man with property.

MRS BENNET *Local* property.

ELIZABETH They are waiting to see if she requires a doctor! I'm going over.

> **ELIZABETH** *takes a coat from coat stand. Rings a bell for a* **SERVANT**, *motions to be brought shoes.*

MR BENNET Dear Eliza there is no horse, Jane took him yesterday.

MRS BENNET Change that dress, wear Sunday's? Mr Darcy will be there and much as I detest him it may result that if *you* stay, if your sister is *very* sick then—

ELIZABETH Leave me out of your dealings, look how they have rewarded poor Jane.

MR BENNET It is three miles, you'll not manage—

MRS BENNET I cannot be held accountable for the rain.

> **MRS BENNET** *does a little thank you to heaven.* **SERVANT** *re-enters with boots, helps* **ELIZABETH** *into them.*

ELIZABETH Concern for my sister will lead my legs Papa.

MRS BENNET Don't try and stop her, she will be propelled by her own stubbornness.

MR BENNET Send over if you need anything, and with news, and what the doctor advises.

MRS BENNET All my girls in male company, it's quite extraordinary!

MARY I think we're forgetting something.

> *Everyone looks at* **MARY**.

I believe I asked for that envelope?

ELIZABETH *hands the paper to* **MARY** *and kisses her as she leaves.* **MARY** *rushes out clutching the envelope.* **MR** *and* **MRS BENNET** *resume eating for a few moments.*

MR BENNET You must obey me in future.

MRS BENNET I will. In the future. Once they are matched.

Scene Seven: Lizzy At Netherfield

MR DARCY, MR BINGLEY, MRS HURST *and* MISS BINGLEY
sit around a table playing cards.

MISS BINGLEY Brother? Brother, please finish your turn.

MR BINGLEY My apologies, I thought I heard something.

MISS BINGLEY She's fine.

MR BINGLEY Perhaps I should go check.

MRS HURST The lady is in bed.

MISS BINGLEY There's nothing to be done, you must stop being
so distracted *at once* and concentrate on the pleasures in
hand.

MR DARCY *(to* MISS BINGLEY*)* I am two rounds from
embarrassing you completely, let us not rush *that*
pleasure.

MISS BINGLEY You may be in for an awful shock Mr Confidence.

MR DARCY I hope so – it would be a delightful change to feel
something that isn't victory.

MRS HURST *(to* MR BINGLEY*)* Will you instruct your friend to
control his arrogance? I swear his attitude is the reason
my hand goes to—

BINGLEY *is staring towards the door again. They all
look at him. It is a few moments before he notices.*

MR BINGLEY When one has a bad cold, it is so bad.

MISS BINGLEY Fancy not sending her in a carriage.

MRS HURST Why did she not turn back with the rain?

MISS BINGLEY Too polite, the peppercorn.

MRS HURST I like her.

MISS BINGLEY *I* like her.

MRS HURST Poor thing.

MISS BINGLEY Do they even have a carriage?

MRS HURST One does not like to ask.

MISS BINGLEY Riding over on a farm horse! Can you imagine?

MR DARCY Not if I hadn't seen it with my own eyes.

MRS HURST My heartfelt sympathy is reserved for her future.

MR BINGLEY How do you mean?

MRS HURST She is such a mild and personable maid.

MISS BINGLEY The prettiest native in the district.

MR DARCY Present company excluded.

MISS BINGLEY I said "native".

MR DARCY My apologies.

MR BINGLEY She is most exceptionally beautiful.

    MISS BINGLEY *and* **MRS HURST** *exchange a look.*

MRS HURST Which is why I feel like crying.

MISS BINGLEY When one imagines the impoverished spinsterhood awaiting her - oh I do so hope...that *we* are not here to see it.

MR BINGLEY But she could win a million hearts!

MRS HURST Surely, if she were from any *other* family—

MISS BINGLEY Even with her poverty—

MRS HURST ...and, one presumes, weak constitution, what with getting colds all the time...

MISS BINGLEY Anything else would be overcome. But those relatives! I cannot bear thinking about them.

MRS HURST Let us not.

    Beat.

MRS HURST Did you hear that their uncle in Cheapside is a butcher?

MISS BINGLEY The London relative of which they are so proud!

MRS HURST And in Cheapside of all places.

MISS BINGLEY If I were Jane I would curl up and die.

MR BINGLEY A butcher?

MR DARCY A—

As **MR DARCY** *tries to speak, the doors swing open and reveal* **ELIZABETH**. *She is soaking and muddy and her hair flies around and she looks ecstatic.*

ELIZABETH I'm dripping like a cloud!

All four of them stare at her. **MR DARCY** *and* **MR BINGLEY** *stand.*

I am here to see my sister.

MRS HURST Perhaps you might like to dry off first by the... Shall I call for a servant?

ELIZABETH No need. If you could direct me to the—

MR BINGLEY You must be ever so worried. We all are.

ELIZABETH Where is she?

MR DARCY If you'd taken the time to write we could have sent you a carriage?

ELIZABETH Nonsense.

MRS HURST *whispers to* **MISS BINGLEY** *who laughs.*

MRS HURST Did you walk the *whole* way?

MISS BINGLEY *(pointed, aimed at* **MR DARCY***)* How bright your eyes from the exertion.

ELIZABETH I will continue with my ramble if you kindly tell me where I may find my—

JANE (*offstage, weak and feeble*) Could it be? Is that Lizzy?

ELIZABETH Coming...

> ELIZABETH *marches out leaving the doors open.*
> MISS BINGLEY *and* MRS HURST *share glances.* MR DARCY
> *looks at* MR BINGLEY, *who is staring at the table.*

MR BINGLEY I wish I was permitted to check on her.

MRS HURST Sir!

MISS BINGLEY She is a-bed!

MR BINGLEY Jane being here, and yet not in my company, I believe I miss her! Do you think I am becoming quite attached?

> MISS BINGLEY *rises and goes over to slam the door shut.*

MISS BINGLEY What the—?!

MRS HURST A complete absence of manners.

MISS BINGLEY Outright rudeness.

MRS HURST Looking like, a kind of, some sort of mermaid medusa.

MISS BINGLEY You are exactly right.

MRS HURST (*to* MR DARCY) Did you see the mud on her skirts and underskirts?

MR DARCY Indeed, I did.

BINGLEY She was worried about dear Jane and—

MISS BINGLEY ...dragged the countryside through our hallway and up the stairs.

MRS HURST I am speechless.

MISS BINGLEY As am I.

MRS HURST I am dumbfounded.

MISS BINGLEY I don't have the words.

MRS HURST They must raise them like wolfhounds over at Longbourn. A big dish of food twice a day and leave them to it.

MISS BINGLEY *(to* **MR DARCY***)* Even your "ardour" must have cooled at such a sight?

MR DARCY I am thinking.

MRS HURST You mustn't think silently.

MISS BINGLEY How cruel.

MRS HURST If you don't think aloud how will anyone know how thoughtful you are?

MISS BINGLEY I insist you tell us what you are thinking.

MR DARCY Perhaps my friend will help me out here?

MR BINGLEY If I can.

MR DARCY I am suddenly struck by something, that perhaps we are respecting – and expecting the wrong things of the gentler sex.

MISS BINGLEY Should we be covered in mud?

MR BINGLEY Continue, I'm intrigued.

MR DARCY All we ever hear about all the women that we know, is how accomplished they are – whether it be musicality, a penchant for reading, a little French...

MRS HURST Oui monsieur.

MR DARCY Was there not something about Miss Bennet when she arrived, some light – a...is this the correct word – dynamism?

MR BINGLEY There was, I agree.

MISS BINGLEY She looked like she had been dragged from the Thames.

MRS HURST I knew she reminded me of someone. That suicide we saw at Wandsworth.

MISS BINGLEY With the recent lack of good company, I believe the gentlemen have become completely insane – the sooner we are back to town the better.

ELIZABETH *enters. She closes the door behind her after a look from* MISS BINGLEY. *There is a moment's silence as she walks towards the table.*

MR BINGLEY How is the patient?

ELIZABETH Trying to sleep. She is sicker than I expected.

MISS BINGLEY Would you like us to arrange a carriage home?

MR DARCY Shall we call for the apothecary?

ELIZABETH The doctor should see her – if she were to worsen then...

MR BINGLEY I'll arrange it now.

MR BINGLEY *jumps up and leaves the room.*

MRS HURST You must let us help you home.

ELIZABETH I will not refuse your assistance.

MISS BINGLEY You're more than welcome, I can't imagine how I would cope if my family didn't have a carriage.

ELIZABETH Most grateful.

MR BINGLEY *enters.*

MR BINGLEY Doctor summoned and I listened at the door – I'm sure she is asleep!

ELIZABETH Thank you for your concern Sir.

MR BINGLEY Would you stay with us? Until she is well enough to move?

ELIZABETH Oh yes, oh thank you – I am most worried you see.

MR BINGLEY I am most worried also.

MISS BINGLEY (*false*) Yes, I am so worried.

MRS HURST *(false)* I am so worried.

Awkward silence as they all look at each other. **MR DARCY** *is staring straight ahead.*

MISS BINGLEY Shall we finish our game?

MR DARCY Care to join us?

ELIZABETH I won't.

MRS HURST It doesn't work with five.

ELIZABETH Thank you. It is fine – I would rather read until my sister wakes.

ELIZABETH *wanders over to a couch. There are four or five books on the table. She picks the top one and sits and opens it.*

MR BINGLEY I'm embarrassed at how few books I can offer you.

MISS BINGLEY Miss Bennet is not here for reading brother.

MR BINGLEY I haven't thought to install a library yet.

MRS HURST Who knows how often we'll even be here?

MR DARCY *(to* **ELIZABETH***)* Do you enjoy reading?

ELIZABETH I should enjoy it right now if permitted.

MR DARCY I can never be sure if... Well, when a woman raises a book to her eyes, I am never convinced if it is the reading she loves, or rather the lady loves being *seen* reading?

ELIZABETH To read for the benefit of other people would be as absurd as—

MISS BINGLEY Darcy is quite concerned with the accomplishments of ladies today.

MRS HURST Or the lack of them.

ELIZABETH *makes a noise of exasperation.*

MISS BINGLEY Excuse us Miss Bennet? Have you *another* opinion to express?

ELIZABETH There is no such thing as female accomplishment if her skill or endeavour is notable merely on account of her sex. A man enjoys playing Beethoven; he has a hobby. A lady sits down to the piano, stumbles through eight bars and it is perceived as achievement because so little was ever expected of her.

MR DARCY *stands up energetically.*

MR DARCY That is what I have been trying to say!

ELIZABETH *(to* **MR DARCY***)* Are you mocking me with false agreement?

MR DARCY *(to* **ELIZABETH***)* You judge my character harshly.

MRS HURST Why, every woman I know is accomplished.

MISS BINGLEY Perhaps Miss Bennet has been moving in lesser circles...?

Sound effects a bell rings offstage. **ELIZABETH** *gets up and takes the book with her.*

ELIZABETH Jane is calling.

MR BINGLEY Send our best.

MISS BINGLEY/MRS HURST *(false)* Lovely to have you here/Let the servants know if you require anything.

ELIZABETH *exits.* **MR DARCY** *stares after her.*

MISS BINGLEY Nothing quite so horrid as a woman who hates other women.

Scene Eight: Collins At Longbourn

MR BENNET *and* MRS BENNET *at the table as before.*
KITTY *wanders in.*

MR BENNET Did you hear that? My stomach!

KITTY Don't be disgusting!

MRS BENNET You're a monster!

MR BENNET I have exciting news.

Sound effects horse and carriage. MRS BENNET *screams and goes to answer to the door.*

KITTY The Captain! You've visited Mr Wickham as we asked?

MR BENNET Am I a battlefield? Or may I be permitted one minute without the appearance of soldiers?

MRS BENNET *re-enters, holding on to a weak* JANE, ELIZABETH *and* LYDIA *follow behind.*

MRS BENNET Must you come so quickly home?

JANE I am repaired mother, I am quite strong.

MR BENNET HURRAH! A sight for sore eyes! And just in time.

ELIZABETH *kisses her father and sits.* JANE *and* MRS BENNET *sit also, a bell is rung and a* SERVANT *enters and sets more places under the following.* MARY *enters and goes to sit at a piano rather than the table.*

I have some most interesting news.

MRS BENNET HUSH sir, it is not your news anyone is interested in. *(to* JANE) How is Mr Bingley?

JANE He is quite well.

MARY *begins to play, the song is unrecognisable and horrific.*

MR BENNET *(to* MARY*)* Stop that this instant.

MARY I have provoked emotion, and will desist. The musician's work is done.

MRS BENNET *(to* JANE*)* And...?

ELIZABETH Everybody at Netherfield is on fine form and sends their regards, Mother. What news here?

KITTY There is a fine new Officer.

LYDIA He'll be Lieutenant.

KITTY Wait 'til you see him.

ELIZABETH *(sarcastic)* I cannot.

MR BENNET We must set another place for lunch.

> MRS BENNET *screams.*

What is this woman?

MRS BENNET You have all been tricking me, is the gentleman coming over?

MR BENNET Yes, he is.

> MRS BENNET *leans over and hugs* JANE. MARY *moves back towards the table.*

MRS BENNET Clever girl, clever rain.

MARY Did she win a painting competition?

MRS BENNET Everybody take your places and act like you don't expect—

JANE Expect what Mother? Father? What is—

MRS BENNET He is coming, Mr Bingley – this can only mean—

> JANE *gets up to look from the window.* KITTY *and* LYDIA *also rush to look.*

MR BENNET Is he? We'll not have space.

MRS BENNET You just this second said—

MR BENNET I didn't—

JANE There is no one coming.

MRS BENNET Poor child. Your father has disappointed us. Again.

MR BENNET And now for my news. I have invited a certain young man to lunch.

MRS BENNET Stop fooling me!

KITTY and LYDIA rush back to the window.

LYDIA There *is* someone coming!

MRS BENNET This is it, the moment a Mother waits for, let me savour every second.

MR BENNET We have never met before, but he sent me such a long and well-mannered letter.

MARY Where is the envelope?

JANE Please Mama, I don't think—

MR BENNET He wanted to make contact. To meet the girls, to—

LYDIA It's a man!

KITTY A sad man!

LYDIA Even his horse is sad.

MARY rushes to the window.

MARY A sad horse?

ELIZABETH Who is coming Papa?

MR BENNET My cousin...

Sound effects door knocker.

MRS BENNET NO...

MR BENNET Mr Collins...

MRS BENNET He mustn't...

MR BENNET ...he is a kindly young fellow, just five and twenty, a Vicar and—

MRS BENNET ...the *creature* that stands to inherit this house and turn my daughters out on the streets and HOW DARE HE show his face here?

MR COLLINS pokes his head around the door at this precise second.

MR COLLINS I've just been admiring your hallway.

MRS BENNET I bet you have.

MR COLLINS Such incredible glass in the door, so that the light on the carpets – woah!

MRS BENNET *(grudging)* Thank you.

MR COLLINS Surely you didn't decorate yourself?

MRS BENNET Why – yes.

MR COLLINS slow claps as he enters the room fully, while nodding his head.

MR COLLINS May I come in and admire the rest of your handiwork?

MRS BENNET Of course, of course.

MR COLLINS Woah again, these beautiful women are your daughters...?

MRS BENNET Stand up ladies.

ELIZABETH, MARY, LYDIA, KITTY and JANE all stand up politely. MR COLLINS slow claps again.

MR COLLINS Stunning. Each and every one.

MRS BENNET Well really...

MR COLLINS I attest, seriously. What beauty. I don't know why people don't say so.

MRS BENNET Well I am sure they do.

MR COLLINS I never heard—

MRS BENNET The eldest Jane is well received of compliments in the area.

MR COLLINS Eldest is "Jane". And I believe all are un-betrothed, all...available?

MRS BENNET Unfortunately...

MR COLLINS Let us have no awkwardness.

MR BENNET Have something to eat. Sit.

The girls sit down. **MR COLLINS** *approaches* **MR BENNET** *and shakes his hand solemnly.*

MR COLLINS We shall not continue with the quarrels of our fathers.

MR BENNET Indeed not. I'm afraid we've only a—

MR COLLINS What a spread. I want to taste everything. I am used to eating the best food as I am regularly entertained by Lady Catherine, Lady Catherine De Bourgh. What a woman.

MR COLLINS *begins loading up his plate. Then catches himself, passes it to* **JANE**. *She puts some food on it as he speaks.*

I'll be describing your hallway to her in detail, she will be interested in your home, your wonderful furniture.

MRS BENNET We own the furniture – it will not be staying.

MR COLLINS I hope that *some* things will...

JANE *passes* **MR COLLINS** *his plate back while trying to avoid his pointed gaze.*

It was Lady Catherine who advised I marry. Our homes are only separated by a garden, mine is much humbler of course – but eventually...

MR COLLINS *shoves some bread in his mouth and chews passionately. The others pick at their food, place small morsels on their plates but mainly watch him.*

This is so delicious it belongs in an asylum. To whom amongst you may I pay my compliments?

MRS BENNET To the cook. Whom we employ. We are not quite so lowly as you seem to find us?

MR COLLINS Not so lowly at all. I wonder, can your daughters cook, especially "Jane". I believe if there is to be a marriage, the correct thing would be for the eldest to—

MRS BENNET Jane is currently being courted – she has an understanding. Very nearly...

JANE *looks visibly relieved.*

MR COLLINS Whom is the second eldest?

MRS BENNET Elizabeth.

ELIZABETH *cringes and stares at her plate.*

MR COLLINS And hardly much less beautiful.

Sound effects horses.

MRS BENNET Why he misses her already! Our proposal is—

MR BENNET What is this now?

MRS BENNET Everybody act normal!

A handsome man in a bright red military jacket is shown into the dining room. **LYDIA** *and* **KITTY** *knock over their chairs in their excitement to get up.* **MR WICKHAM** *bows very, very deeply.*

MR WICKHAM I am afraid I have done something impatient and most terribly rude.

MRS BENNET *flushes and nudges* **MR BENNET** *who stands.*

MR BENNET How may we help you sir?

MR WICKHAM I have come to present myself, Sir. I, and those in my command, will be local for near to three months and having become acquainted with your daughters of late, I thought I should visit to commend the man who raised them.

LYDIA/KITTY *(swoony)* Ooh/oh my...

MRS BENNET What manners!

MR BENNET You have saved me a...a journey—

MR WICKHAM I apologise for my timing, if you'll allow me to wait in the hallway.

MR COLLINS Isn't it lovely?

MRS BENNET Nonsense, you'll join us and tell us all about yourself and your "hopes" and—

LYDIA Sit next to me!

> **MR WICKHAM** *takes a chair between* **ELIZABETH** *and* **LYDIA***. As he sits* **ELIZABETH** *leans towards him.*

ELIZABETH You will never learn how grateful I am for your entrance.

MR WICKHAM I hope that is not true – for I hope to learn *everything* there is to know about you.

MR COLLINS I'd love to read a short sermon if I may?

> *As* **MR COLLINS** *speaks he rummages through his bag looking for the book.*

Lady Catherine enjoys religious readings a whole lot more than her attendance at church would suggest, so when I am invited to attend her, sometimes once or even – no, once on a weekly basis, she will persuade me to perform a reading or two. But usually one, although I flatter myself it is also my companionship she enjoys. Ah here it is – it involves a goat, do the little ones like goats?

MR COLLINS *looks expectantly at* **KITTY** *and* **LYDIA.**

(pointed) This is for your benefit. Goats have an abundance of energy. Like some other creatures, I might mention...

MARY Poor Lizzy.

MR COLLINS "Favour is deceitful. Unlike sobriety, which is a virtue."

MR WICKHAM *(to* **ELIZABETH***)* Did your cousin refer to Lady Catherine De Bourgh?

ELIZABETH Only seventeen times so far.

MR COLLINS "...with spindly legs and excitable constitutions, the fellows are known for taking on the most treacherous mountains. But God gives horns for a reason – and that reason is unreasonable—"

Did I mention I wrote this myself?

"When a goat is unreasonable, what this means is that the mountain will tire of his spindly legs and want to cast him asunder. And what relevance does this confer upon us?"

MR WICKHAM How well does he know her?

ELIZABETH Their acquaintance is recent, as she found him his position, but I do not know how they became known – are you familiar with the Lady, is she quite as pompous as Mr Collins describes?

MR WICKHAM She is aunt to an acquaintance of mine.

ELIZABETH Please forgive me, I was completely out of turn, out of sorts, I had not heard of Lady Catherine's existence before today and was flippant.

MR WICKHAM Please do not apologise, this acquaintance is not... I am not on friendly terms with...

LYDIA He means Darcy. They hate each other.

MR COLLINS *raises voice to regain* **LYDIA***'s attention.*

MR COLLINS "If a maid forgets her ornaments, this would be like a bride without her gown and veil. And the congregation would be...!"

I really believe analogy is one of my real strengths, if we could all pay attention.

"The congregation would be shocked at the maid's very person and any union would be deemed a joke and an undoing of any decent and hardworking young man. Thus it is also thus with comportment, it is no good being a daughter of kings with a dress of spun gold, if inside the princess, all along was a little grey goat."

MR COLLINS *stops and looks at every one. They look unsurely at each other.* **MR WICKHAM** *starts a round of applause and bows at* **MR COLLINS**.

MR WICKHAM You are absolutely correct in your assessment of yourself and your strengths of analogy. Perhaps we might test how much our young friends were listening, with a civilised game of cards?

MR COLLINS I am against games for young women on principle, but as this is a test...

MR BENNET I am still eating.

LYDIA Papa has gout.

MR WICKHAM Why play at cards, when the best entertainment of all is sitting to our left and right?

KITTY *and* **MARY** *look disappointedly left and right at their mother and then each other.*

The witty words of these outrageously attractive, well-bred women.

MRS BENNET Thank you, Mr W—

MR COLLINS *(interrupting)* And their mother.

MRS BENNET *looks furious.*

(*to* ELIZABETH) I am very good at compliments. Which is compliment to myself I suppose. Proving my point.

MR WICKHAM (*rescuing* ELIZABETH) You are used to high society Sir, you are everything I am not, and the gentleman I wish to be.

MR BENNET I have lost my appetite.

MR BENNET *rises from the table and sets off a flurry of motion.* LYDIA *and* KITTY *run to set up a card table,* MR COLLINS *follows them reading excerpts from his sermon book.* MRS BENNET *instructs the stagehand/* SERVANTs *as they remove dishes from the table.* JANE *sits for* MARY *to sketch her, but* MARY *will wander off before the end of the scene.* MR WICKHAM *and* ELIZABETH *remain at the table.*

MR WICKHAM May I be permitted to speak with you a moment?

ELIZABETH You may.

MR WICKHAM I wish to speak frankly.

ELIZABETH I consider honest speech a virtue.

MR WICKHAM When I met with your charming sisters in town a few days ago, we conversed at length about the area and, there was mention of the eldest Miss Bennet taken ill.

ELIZABETH As you can see, she is much recovered.

MR WICKHAM I am deeply relieved.

ELIZABETH Does this concern Mr Darcy?

MR WICKHAM This is difficult for me. Pardon my impertinence. I was made aware as to your whereabouts and was shocked to discover that Mr Darcy found himself in the district when I... I am doing my best to keep a long, long way from his... Excuse me.

MR WICKHAM *is distraught.*

ELIZABETH You know Mr Bingley also?

MR WICKHAM I do not. From everything I hear he is quite the most remarkably cheerful fellow.

ELIZABETH He is delightful, sunshine in a man.

MR WICKHAM Which makes it unfathomable that he keeps company with... Everybody is fooled by Darcy. He knows who to charm and whom he may...

ELIZABETH He has not charmed me. I believe from the outset I could judge Mr Darcy in exactly his true spirit.

MR WICKHAM He is a snob.

ELIZABETH He is proud.

MR WICKHAM And cruel.

ELIZABETH He judges snidely.

MR WICKHAM ...but only those he considers beneath him—

ELIZABETH ...which is everyone.

> **LYDIA** *and* **KITTY** *come over.*

LYDIA Have you told her?

MR WICKHAM I am enjoying quite the warmest meeting of minds.

KITTY Mr Darcy stole his money.

LYDIA And that's why he must be a soldier.

ELIZABETH What is this?

> **MRS BENNET** *and* **MR COLLINS** *are now listening as well.*

MR WICKHAM I had intended follow my calling into the church...

MR COLLINS Hallelujah!

MR WICKHAM And my Godfather left me a generous amount per year in order that I might do so.

MR COLLINS Thanks be unto his goodness.

MR WICKHAM This of course was Mr Darcy senior, he bequeathed me a living and property. But after his sad passing his intentions were ignored, the stipend named for me was used – elsewhere.

MRS BENNET The rotten scoundrel!

ELIZABETH We know Mr Darcy to be rude, but surely no one is so hard as this?

LYDIA He is jealous.

KITTY *(to* **MR WICKHAM***)* Jealous because you are handsomer.

MR WICKHAM No...

MRS BENNET Yes!

MR WICKHAM He is envious of his late father's affections. If the senior had loved me a little less, the younger would not loathe me so much now.

ELIZABETH This is so much for me to absorb and make meaning of...

MR WICKHAM Then you can imagine how I feel.

ELIZABETH I do believe I can.

Scene Nine: Edit Suite

Lights dim and everybody on stage freezes.

FEMALE VOICE *(offstage)* That's it – and we freeze there. On her eyes as they look upwards at him.

MALE VOICE *(offstage)* Do we want him in shot?

FEMALE VOICE *(offstage)* It's not his story – we don't care about him, how he feels.

MALE VOICE *(offstage)* No need to snap. We're getting there.

FEMALE VOICE *(offstage)* I wasn't snapping. I was answering your question.

Lights focus on a small area on the front of stage that has become a booth full of monitors. If there can be film projections onto the set that would be preferable. In booth, **MODERN MARY** *and* **GRAHAM**.

GRAHAM The Wickham guy is so charming here – I think *I'm* in love with him.

MODERN MARY He's gorgeous.

GRAHAM *(jealous)* He's gay in real life...

MODERN MARY stares at GRAHAM like "What's your point?"

I want to go back and check we've made Darcy sympathetic enough?

MODERN MARY He isn't sympathetic.

GRAHAM Shouldn't he be?

MODERN MARY Why?

GRAHAM So that, you know, it's a bloody love story.

MODERN MARY Maybe it's a history lesson.

GRAHAM They've filmed a love story. It will be advertised as a love story. I'll lose my job if we deliver some bitter spinster propaganda.

MODERN MARY Wow.

GRAHAM I think we were wrong to cut the drawing room moment – you know, when Miss Bingley is playing and Darcy asks Lizzy to dance.

MODERN MARY It's pointless.

GRAHAM It shows he likes her, that he is... Hang on let me find it...

Sound effects ballroom music, spotlight on ELIZABETH *watching a dancefloor,* MR DARCY *approaches.*

MR DARCY I should say this music would inspire you to dance a fling?

ELIZABETH I am sure that is what you would *like* me to say, then you could reprimand me on my poor taste and timing but I assure you I fancy no dance, and no judgement.

Music stops, spotlight darkens. Back to booth.

MODERN MARY Yeah, wow. Can't lose that magical moment of romance.

GRAHAM He's trying... He's awkward.

MODERN MARY You marry him.

GRAHAM It's her that's spikey.

GRAHAM *types into the computer, scans through images.*

What about that moment when he can't take his eyes off her? She's walking with Miss Bingley...

Spotlight on MR DARCY *watching* ELIZABETH.

MODERN MARY I mean, who goes for a walk IN A ROOM?

GRAHAM It was a different time. It was...you know, a time of room walking...

MARY Can we do a flashback? I'll mock one up so that during his proposal later, when the viewers are swooning into their ready meals, I'll remind them what he said after this broody staring.

MR DARCY *holds a tea cup to his lips, and then speaks instead of drinking.*

MR DARCY Even with her teasing, or perhaps because of it, I find myself attracted to her more than I would like. I must endeavour that no sign of admiration escapes me, or she will grow hopeful of a match such that could never be made between myself and someone so lowly.

MODERN MARY He's an arsehole.

GRAHAM Is this about what happened with you and—

MODERN MARY *(quickly)* Jane doesn't speak enough. We need to want her to be happy – who is she?

GRAHAM Can't we talk?

MODERN MARY And what is the weird one doing with those envelopes?

Scene Ten: Netherfield Ball

Sound effects trumpet.

MALE VOICE *(offstage)* Colonel E. Great!

Trumpet sound effects.

Sergeant Stewart Middle!

Hall forms at Netherfield. Cardboard cut outs of Soldiers make the stage seem busier. Trumpet sound effects.

MR and MRS Phillips!

ELIZABETH *and* **JANE** *stand at the front of the stage, there is much movement and greeting behind them.* **ELIZABETH** *is looking towards the door. Trumpet sound effects.*

MR and MRS Lucas!

JANE This is so unlike you.

ELIZABETH Pardon me?

JANE Distracted by thoughts of a man.

ELIZABETH I don't know how you can bear it. It's so consuming.

JANE I fight it with a nagging and constant thought, I tell myself over and again that I am not special, not worthy and *he* will soon realise.

ELIZABETH But you are special.

JANE To my sister...

ELIZABETH If I had a choice of all the sisters in the world I could not select a woman of better wisdom and character. You are such good company! You cheer me and entertain me and—

JANE I did not come fishing for compliments. I am merely telling you how I keep my heart in my chest when all she wants is to fly away and batter herself against another's.

ELIZABETH Why not fly and—?

JANE This is not a book Lizzy. You know why. I do allow myself my pleasures, when he is near I—

JANE *looks around and checks where* **MR BINGLEY** *is in the room.*

ELIZABETH Do you love him?

JANE Ssshh. That is the word we cannot afford. But when he is near, when we dance or eat or talk - then I permit myself, if not *flight* - then the *glow*. His smile and eyes and, watching his fingers. Silly girl that I am.

ELIZABETH My sister! You are brave!

JANE They won't allow it. His sisters—

ELIZABETH He will resist them.

JANE No. Lizzy, our contentment must arise from the pleasures we control.

Trumpet sound effects. **ELIZABETH** *turns once again and is disappointed.*

MALE VOICE *(offstage)* Mistress Sedgwick!

JANE It is Wickham that distracts you?

ELIZABETH I think of him! I think of him so fondly and I am so sad about his disinheritance and I want so badly to—

JANE It is not your business.

ELIZABETH It is SO UNFAIR! This sweet, caring gentleman who wants for so little - an enemy of a haughty princeling who by birth was gifted wherewithal to control another's fate, to throw it in the dustbin!

JANE We are not in possession of every detail.

MR BINGLEY *approaches the sisters.*

MR BINGLEY I kept my promise! A ball at Netherfield to appease your sisters. And another promise, one that I made to myself. Will you dance the first two with your host? I would be honoured...

JANE (*coolly*) Of course, this is lovely you know.

MR BINGLEY Thank you

JANE Thank *you*.

BINGLEY *and* **JANE** *dance away, and then subtly exit.*
MRS BENNET *and* **MARY** *join* **ELIZABETH**.

MRS BENNET May I leave her with you? I am trying to ascertain if Mr Wickham has arrived.

MARY And I keep telling you, I have no idea.

ELIZABETH Of course, my sister...

MARY But I did see someone in a red jacket...

MRS BENNET *walks quickly away.*

ELIZABETH Did you know Mary, that a mule is a cross between a donkey and a horse?

MARY I don't know if I agree.

ELIZABETH *smiles at her sister. They are approached from behind by* **MR COLLINS**.

MR COLLINS A fine occasion for socialising.

ELIZABETH I'm glad you approve cousin.

MR COLLINS I more than approve. Or rather, I exactly approve.

ELIZABETH You will meet some lovely gentlefolk from around the district.

MARY The mule has no right to be cross.

MR COLLINS I am looking at a lovely Lady – I am sure Jane will understand, as *understandings* are made.

MARY What the horse gets up to is no business of his.

MR COLLINS May I have the pleasure of the first two dances with my second choice?

ELIZABETH *looks towards the door. And then back to* **MR COLLINS.** *What can she do?* **MARY** *claps.*

ELIZABETH I'd be most grateful.

MR COLLINS *and* **ELIZABETH** *dance awkwardly as she tries to keep physically distant from him. Choreography and music should suggest time moving, at the end of two dances (a minute real time), as* **ELIZABETH** *attempts to escape* **MR COLLINS** *she is approached by* **MR DARCY.**

MR DARCY *(stiff)* If I may, I come in application of your hand.

ELIZABETH *(surprised but polite)* Why! Yes of course.

MR COLLINS *is excited.* **ELIZABETH** *and* **MR DARCY** *stand looking at each other while he speaks.*

MR COLLINS Sir you have ended my quest, my name is Collins I am known, I am most *grateful* to be known to your aunt Lady Catherine – Lady Catherine De Bourgh. A fine woman, the *finest.* I dine with her almost once a...fortnight at her lodgings, and, OH she is full of advice and helpfulness as you yourself must know. She helped me a great deal with my plumbing.

ELIZABETH *(to* **MR DARCY***)* Are you to compliment me on my dancing?

MR DARCY Your dancing was perfectly competent.

MR COLLINS I usually cannot abide the evils of a ball, I don't like to mention Lucifer on a pretty night such as this but, there you go, wherever there is music and young people he is also invited. But tonight, I am glad I have attended not merely as a chaperone but, as a suitor.

MR COLLINS *looks meaningfully at* **ELIZABETH.**

ELIZABETH *(to* MR DARCY*)* I believe we too have a mutual acquaintance.

MR DARCY Ah...

ELIZABETH A Mr Wickham has been stationed in our district.

MR DARCY Word had reached me of his being in the locality.

ELIZABETH I found him to be most charming.

MR DARCY You did.

ELIZABETH I was expecting to find him present this evening with his regiment.

MR DARCY I am sorry your wishes were disappointed. Mr Wickham is indeed a—

MR COLLINS ...very, very handsome man.

ELIZABETH And most sympathetic. He explained his "situation".

MR DARCY I doubt he enlightened you fully...

ELIZABETH I can assure you I know *everything*.

Music begins, couples begin to form again on the floor.

MR COLLINS I shall leave you in my cousin's surprisingly firm arms. Obliged to make your acquaintance Mr Darcy, and congratulations to your friend in snaring the most attractive of the Bennet sisters!

MR DARCY *reacts to what* MR COLLINS *has said.* MR COLLINS *walks away and* MR DARCY *looks down at* ELIZABETH. *She looks sad.*

ELIZABETH I must apologise for the excitement of my relative.

MR DARCY *looks around and notices* JANE *and* MR BINGLEY *are nowhere to be seen.*

MR DARCY I must find my friend, please excuse me.

MR DARCY walks away. CHARLOTTE joins ELIZABETH to watch him leave.

ELIZABETH Oh Charlotte...

CHARLOTTE Am I mistaken, or did the richest man here ask you to dance?

ELIZABETH I care not for his wealth, especially while knowing that a sum of it was due to another. A man who cannot show his face here in case it engenders further cruelties.

CHARLOTTE Will you judge me awful if *I* continue to care for his wealth? You'll introduce me when he returns?

CHARLOTTE and ELIZABETH watch as JANE and MR BINGLEY re-enter, they are almost holding hands. MR DARCY speaks to them tensely.

ELIZABETH I fear dancing is no longer on his mind.

CHARLOTTE Why on earth did he ask?

ELIZABETH It is a mystery. Perhaps he wished me to tread on his toes or whisper some faux pas that he could repeat with his friends later.

CHARLOTTE You think this poorly of him?

JANE approaches.

JANE There is some tension between the gentlemen. You didn't mention Mr Wickham?

ELIZABETH Indeed, I did. A person should know when news of their actions has travelled. Perhaps this way even the rich will realise their behaviour has a consequence.

JANE You are becoming quite foolish over Wickham.

CHARLOTTE Is he really that handsome?

ELIZABETH *(to JANE)* The complete opposite, I have become quite sensible to injustice and those who commit it.

JANE Charles said, excuse me, Mr Bingley told me that—

CHARLOTTE It is Charles now? You have an...arrangement?

JANE *(firm)* Mr Bingley...

ELIZABETH Does he know Wickham?

JANE He is quite sure the inheritance was conditional only and that the conditions were breached.

ELIZABETH Nonsense. Or else Mr Wickham would have said.

CHARLOTTE Why you even flush to say his name... You *are* foolish for him.

ELIZABETH I redden with fury.

JANE This is not our concern.

> MISS BINGLEY *approaches the women and they awkwardly go silent. Only* JANE *remains friendly.*

MISS BINGLEY My beautiful friend...

> JANE *and* MISS BINGLEY *embrace.*

JANE Are you having a wonderful time? It is so kind of your brother to treat us to such a delightful ball.

CHARLOTTE Yes.

ELIZABETH It is lovely.

MISS BINGLEY And the perfect send off! We will have such affectionate memories of our stay.

JANE Oh no! You and your sister are leaving? I'll miss you!

MISS BINGLEY We will miss *you. We* have become so fond. You must write!

JANE I will of course!

MISS BINGLEY And if you are ever in town you must rush to us.

JANE ...I will insist your brother keeps me updated with *all* of your news.

MISS BINGLEY I am afraid his letters are sparsely detailed if, indeed they are ever completed let alone sent.

Beat and reactions.

ELIZABETH Your whole party is to leave the district?

MISS BINGLEY Yes.

JANE When to return?

MISS BINGLEY We have no such plans. It's so sad for me.

JANE *looks around for* **MR BINGLEY**.

My brother has rushed to assist Mr Darcy with some business and has had to leave his own soirée, the squirrel!

JANE He has gone?

MISS BINGLEY Good luck my dearest, dear Jane.

MISS BINGLEY *embraces* **JANE**. **CHARLOTTE** *and* **ELIZABETH** *look at each other and reach out to hold hands.* **MISS BINGLEY** *nods at* **ELIZABETH** *and walk away.* **JANE** *is utterly composed.*

ELIZABETH Shall we—

JANE It is important we stay. For our sisters.

CHARLOTTE Perhaps he will call for you in the morning?

JANE He is a very sweet man. But he is not a brave one.

Scene Eleven: Rehearsals

The girls hold hands and watch the dancing. After a few moments, lights fade. Staging becomes stripped back, as does music. Lights up on **MODERN ELIZABETH**, **MODERN JANE** *and* **MODERN CHARLOTTE** *in same positions, holding scripts with some version of their previous costume.* **MODERN MARY** *sits behind a piano.* **MODERN MRS BENNET** (**MODERN MB**) *has a chair, some water and fruit at her feet and a pen and folder in her hand.*

MODERN JANE Surely we need to see more struggle from her? She is sad, obviously.

MODERN MB She has to be composed.

MODERN JANE She seems like she doesn't care.

MODERN MB This is Regency England.

MODERN JANE They still had emotions. Probably more because there were no distractions. They just stood around in dresses feeling their feelings.

MODERN MB So, feel and repress. But I don't want to see it. Let's imagine that Jane, our Jane is a better actor than you – she has been—

MODERN JANE She hasn't been to LAMDA.

MODERN MB In *life.* Jane is far better at hiding her feelings than you are because she has had to do that ever since she learned to talk because, her time and its expectations dictated—

MODERN ELIZABETH Are we projecting?

MODERN MB We are taking this directly from the text. Austen tells us herself exactly how a woman should behave.

MODERN CHARLOTTE Hmmm.

MODERN ELIZABETH Can we talk about Lizzy? I don't remember her being in love with some soldier.

MODERN MB In the book, it says she can't stop thinking about him.

MODERN ELIZABETH I don't think they put that bit in the film.

MODERN MB He was kind to her, he is handsome.

MODERN JANE I wish we'd got Idris Elba like you wanted.

MODERN ELIZABETH Can you imagine? I'd get to kiss him...

MODERN MB Lizzy doesn't kiss Wickham.

MODERN ELIZABETH We'd add it in.

MODERN CHARLOTTE I prefer Sense and Sensibility...

Everyone looks at **CHARLOTTE.**

...that's the one where you swoon or fall over and a man picks you up and marries you. I think that one is better.

MODERN MB Let's call that lunch.

Scene Twelve: Proposals

Actors exit as **MARY** *enters alone. She sits at piano.*

The Longbourn dining room is built by **SERVANTS** *around her as she plays.* **MRS BENNET** *enters and sits at the table drinking tea.* **ELIZABETH** *enters with a book and sits near her mother.* **MR COLLINS** *enters and shouts over the music.*

MR COLLINS *(shouting)* I wonder if I might request a moment's solitude, only not alone, but with Miss Elizabeth?

> **MARY** *stops playing and stares.* **MRS BENNET** *stands up and almost runs out of the room.*

MRS BENNET Yes!

ELIZABETH No...

MRS BENNET Of course! Congratulations...

ELIZABETH Mother may stay...

MRS BENNET ...on asking...for solitude!

ELIZABETH ...we have no secrets here.

> **MRS BENNET** *drags* **MARY** *and they exit.*

MR COLLINS I begin today with my best intentions.

ELIZABETH —

MR COLLINS As I am sure you are aware, I stand to inherit your home at your father's passing.

ELIZABETH I am aware and, if I am allowed—

MR COLLINS Please do not be melancholy. This may not occur for up to several years. I am to cheer you now, with every young woman's dream. A proposal.

> **MR COLLINS** *looks expectantly at* **ELIZABETH**.

Feel free to cry.

ELIZABETH You are most kind.

MR COLLINS I have decided to get married because it would make me happy, because it is better than getting a dog and because Lady Catherine told me to.

ELIZABETH If I have not misread this situation—

MR COLLINS You are correct. Lady Catherine gives me much advice, and has been most generous in her tips for choosing a bride. She insisted I not opt for highly bred, avoid the overly beautiful and make sure the maid is clever enough to manage my small income. You are perfect.

ELIZABETH Sir, I am sure you flatter me but—

MR COLLINS Get used to it! Flattery is my strong suit! Plenty more where that came from...

Beat.

Your arms are *very* firm.

ELIZABETH Thank you. My cousin, I must cease our conversing as I cannot accept your kind offer.

MR COLLINS Haha, oh yes, I know – a young lady likes to refuse a man she intends to accept all in the fun of getting him to ask again. I'll ask once more this afternoon. Or now, just to get things settled?

ELIZABETH I can assure you I am not, nor do I know of *any* young woman who would risk her happiness by—

MR COLLINS WILL. YOU. MARRY. ME?

ELIZABETH As I recently explained, I cannot, for I—

MR COLLINS Do not be afeard of Lady Catherine, I will put a good word in for you – maybe a whole sentence.

ELIZABETH That is not my reason, my feeling is that I—

MR COLLINS Absolutely, I understand that you must go through with the charade. I will ask again later, maybe teatime?

ELIZABETH Sir, I exhort you—

MR COLLINS I know you would not reject me for I am utterly worthy of you. You're very lucky!

MRS BENNET *bursts through the door,* JANE, MARY *and* LYDIA *follow her looking worried.*

MRS BENNET Congratulations!

MR COLLINS Thank you ever so much.

MRS BENNET What a fantastic start to the day!

MR COLLINS It is very terrific!

ELIZABETH *(to* JANE*)* Everyone is insane.

JANE My sister?

ELIZABETH I have rejected our cousin's kind offer.

JANE *hugs* ELIZABETH *in relief.* MRS BENNET *has heard.*

MRS BENNET *(to* MR COLLINS*)* Did she dare refuse?

MR COLLINS Purely as a female trick, I am quite charmed by her delicacy, I'll ask again after lunch.

MRS BENNET Be assured I will insist she answer more positively.

MR COLLINS Oh no...

MRS BENNET She is a rude and impudent.

MR COLLINS *(quickly)* Then perhaps not a suitable wife? Lady Catherine was quite clear...

MR BENNET *enters.*

MR BENNET Why this racket when a decent man is doing his best to digest his breakfast?

MRS BENNET Your disgrace of a daughter has embarrassed us. Instruct her that she will be unknown to me unless she accepts Mr Collins' hand.

MR BENNET *looks seriously at* **ELIZABETH.**

MR BENNET Whatever decision you make, you risk losing the support of your parents. My wife will never speak to you unless you accept Mr Collins, and neither will I...if you do.

ELIZABETH Papa!

MRS BENNET What an awful father you are, what will she do without...

Sound effects a bell rings as **MRS BENNET** *is shouting.*

...someone to take care of her, what with her terrible attitude – you have fed this fiery temperament.

MR COLLINS I rather think I have changed my mind.

MRS BENNET We have lost him – unless, have you had a good look at Lydia?

LYDIA *looks terrified.* **CHARLOTTE** *is shown in by a* **SERVANT** *and* **LYDIA** *runs to her.*

CHARLOTTE *(whisper)* What is going on?

LYDIA *(whisper)* Our cousin has proposed to Lizzy, she has replied a firm no and Mother is having kittens and will make anyone marry him who moves just so she can keep the house, she doesn't even care that—

CHARLOTTE *(slightly louder)* Mr Collins is the cousin who inherits Longbourn?

MR COLLINS *almost on hearing his name approaches.*

MR COLLINS Welcome Miss Lucas...

LYDIA *runs away from him again, she hides behind* **JANE** *and* **ELIZABETH.**

MRS BENNET I could not be more furious with my two eldest – one for letting her only chance at happiness leave the district...

JANE This was hardly my fault.

MRS BENNET And the other for ensuring my old age will not be spent comfortably in my own home.

ELIZABETH Mother, I am sorry, our situation – our future – but how could I—

MR COLLINS *walks into the centre of the room.*

MR COLLINS Congratulations are in order.

MR BENNET This is pantomime...

ELIZABETH (*frustrated*) I am a reasonable woman, I have been clear and—

MR COLLINS ...I believe I have found myself a most suitable wife.

CHARLOTTE *walks a few steps behind* **MR COLLINS**. *She rests her hand on his arm.*

CHARLOTTE (*smiles*) I cannot *wait* to meet Lady Catherine.

MRS BENNET *faints noisily.*

Scene Thirteen: Back To Rehearsal

Lights change, rehearsal room. **MODERN ELIZABETH** *and* **MODERN JANE** *are holding scripts.*

MODERN JANE *(reading)* "My dear sister, Charlotte is our friend – but surely here she has abused us."

MODERN ELIZABETH *(reading)* "Nonsense, our friend has no taste for marriage or the company of our cousin, but to attain a living has always been her ambition. She has achieved it and deserves our admiration."

MODERN JANE *(reading)* "Do you regret your decision?"

MODERN ELIZABETH *(reading)* "I could not have made any other."

MODERN JANE I believe her, do you? I think—

MODERN MB *rushes in, chucks bag down, tries to find script etc.*

MODERN MB Great – you've started – sorry, my appointment overran, any revelations?

MODERN ELIZABETH The vicar's an idiot and her mate is a bitch.

MODERN JANE They deserve each other.

MODERN MB I was being sarcastic.

MODERN ELIZABETH Liz is in the same position and she turned him down.

MODERN MB *(considering)* She's proud. Elizabeth Bennet does not behave as a woman in her lowly position should – that's why she's interesting.

MODERN JANE I've got another question, when Jane gets the letter out – where is it? In her bra or something?

MODERN MB I think pocket...

MODERN JANE And does she know it by heart? Or read?

MODERN MB Read. I think it'll be really effective if we can hear her sadness at their not planning to return for whole winter, and at hearing that Bingley might be meant for Miss Darcy – sort of pause and swallow on that line – feel her pain at even saying the words.

MODERN ELIZABETH Miss Bingley is the worst.

MODERN JANE This is the line that kills me: "I wish I could hear that you, my dearest friend, had any intention of attending on us in London for we would love to see you. But alas I know that hope to be groundless." She doesn't invite her! Tells her: "Oh it's a shame you can't come to London." Invite her then!

MODERN MB Jane wouldn't think that – she is not presumptuous.

MODERN JANE Of course she would, she just swallows it.

MODERN MB We can try it that way.

MODERN ELIZABETH Thank God those relatives take her to London anyway...

MODERN MB Let's go back and hear this scene from the top...

MODERN ELIZABETH When are we doing the Wickham scenes?

MODERN MB We're working around availabilities so I don't know yet, why?

MODERN ELIZABETH No reason.

Scene Fourteen: Lady Catherine

Lights become dim, figures shadowy. Evocative and soulful music plays. The impressive rooms of **LADY CATHERINE** *are created as* **JANE** *and* **CHARLOTTE** *write/ read letters in spotlights.*

JANE Dearest Lizzy, please write quickly with all the news of the district. I miss everybody wretchedly – despite the kindness of our aunty and uncle. The journey was fine and London so much busier than I could have imagined. Have you seen Wickham? Is he becoming attached? I do so hope that I will hear of a great love when I return! Am I being too romantic again? I wrote to Caroline Bingley – how excited she will be to hear of my surprise arrival against all expectations!

CHARLOTTE Dear Lizzy, thank you for your letter and your kindnesses after my marriage. Will your mother ever forgive me? She considers me as an adopted orphan who has stolen off with her best silver. The house is charming and my days are comfortable. I wish someone could have warned me about the nights. Lady Catherine is a superb woman – write back soon – Mrs Charlotte Collins.

JANE ...no reply from Caroline but Mrs Gardiner explains it is a busy season with balls and socialising. I have plenty to entertain myself, what with writing letters and thinking and reading...

CHARLOTTE ...the little parsonage is well kept. Occasionally I break something for the fun of clearing it up and hiding that I've done it...

JANE Still nothing from my London friends. My letters must've been going astray, I am much cheered by this realisation and my aunt has given me permission to visit there...

CHARLOTTE ...Lady Catherine has been generous enough to share her tips in fighting knotweed, so even that excitement is over...

JANE ...Miss Bingley was civil but only barely. I stayed for twenty minutes, for which whole time she spoke about the young Miss Darcy and her fine breeding and playing. I believe I have misled myself in finding any affection from her towards me...

CHARLOTTE ...my husband is spending today counting the windows of all the houses in the district so that he may mention the number in his next sermon...

JANE ...I think I did not admit what hopes I had, as time passes and... I was silly. I believed he would hear and I was so sure he would come.

CHARLOTTE ...visit soon or I'll drown myself in the pond.

MR COLLINS *enters, he is soon followed by* CHARLOTTE *and* ELIZABETH.

MR COLLINS You must not be flattered the invitation was extended on your account Miss Elizabeth, Lady Catherine condescends to entertain us on a nearly weekly basis. Although, in this instance, you may call yourself fortunate for such an event to take place on the first evening of your visit...

CHARLOTTE *squeezes* ELIZABETH's *hand and mouths* "*Thank You*".

...and you must not feel self-conscious on the style of your dress...

CHARLOTTE *(to* ELIZABETH*)* I am so looking forward to hearing how you find our benefactor.

MR COLLINS ...Lady Catherine believes every person should dress to their place.

CHARLOTTE Lady Catherine has given me such *kind* advice as to the appropriate garments for all occasions.

MR COLLINS The lady will be pleased that your attire makes obvious your lowly social standing.

CHARLOTTE She may even tell you so.

ELIZABETH Oh good.

> *Lights down, gravel and doorbell sound effects and lights up on* **LADY CATHERINE DE BOURGH**'s *drawing room. Seated at the table are* **MR COLLINS, ELIZABETH, CHARLOTTE, LADY CATHERINE,** *her daughter* **MISS DE BOURGH** *looking sickly, cross and covered in a blanket.*

LADY CATHERINE ...I wish you had consulted me as I have only recently counted the windows of the neighbourhood.

MR COLLINS I do not doubt, I would never doubt, your extensive intelligence.

LADY CATHERINE Pah, it was only counting.

MR COLLINS You astound me Madame.

LADY CATHERINE I myself possess ninety-four of the windows.

MR COLLINS And by far the finest...

LADY CATHERINE But of course.

CHARLOTTE By far the finest.

LADY CATHERINE *(obviously)* Yes.

> **LADY CATHERINE** *looks at* **ELIZABETH** *as if expecting something. Small awkward silence.*

MISS DE BOURGH For looking through.

CHARLOTTE You're absolutely correct.

MR COLLINS Most perceptive.

LADY CATHERINE *(to* **ELIZABETH***)* What is your mother's maiden name?

ELIZABETH Why, I believe she was a—

LADY CATHERINE I understand from Mrs Collins you had no governess.

ELIZABETH No indeed, we were encouraged to read and—

LADY CATHERINE I wish I had acquaintance with your mother in order I might scold her on her misconduct toward you and your sisters. Mrs Collins has referred to your all being out at once.

ELIZABETH How flattered I am that my family has taken your notice.

LADY CATHERINE How old are you?

ELIZABETH Excuse me...?

CHARLOTTE She's—

ELIZABETH I am the second eldest, I must be permitted to demure on the exact figure.

LADY CATHERINE You refuse to answer?

Sound effects bell.

MISS DE BOURGH Why, that sounded like our doorbell.

MR COLLINS Well I never.

CHARLOTTE What ears you have!

A **SERVANT** *shows* **MR DARCY** *into the room.* **MR COLLINS** *applauds in excitement.*

LADY CATHERINE My nephew! You are two days early!

MR DARCY You have company?

LADY CATHERINE Hardly—

MR DARCY *appears embarrassed.*

MR DARCY *(to* **CHARLOTTE***)* My congratulations upon your marriage.

CHARLOTTE/LADY CATHERINE Thank you, sir/You have met Mrs Collins earlier?

MR COLLINS We all became merrily acquainted in Hertfordshire.

MISS DE BOURGH *neatly falls asleep in her own lap.*

MR DARCY Hello again.

LADY CATHERINE The young woman with Mrs Collins will not tell me her age.

MR DARCY Good evening Miss Bennet.

ELIZABETH Good Evening Sir.

Lighting change, becomes ethereal. **ELIZABETH** *and* **MR DARCY** *move closer towards each other.*

MR DARCY I trust you have been well?

ELIZABETH I trust you have been well also.

MR DARCY Your family well...also?

ELIZABETH My sister Jane is in London, perhaps you have seen her?

MR DARCY I have not.

Silence. Long silence.

ELIZABETH And your sister is well?

MR DARCY She is.

ELIZABETH You are visiting long with your aunt?

Silence.

It is usual to expect a reply to a—

MR DARCY I heard that a party visited locally. What I mean to say is, your presence here was...

ELIZABETH I am visiting my friend at the Vicarage.

MR DARCY I have... Your whereabouts are... Much to my displeasure... I seem to be aware of you and your...

ELIZABETH Whatever I have done to displease you is—

MR DARCY In vain have I struggled. It will not do. My feelings will not be repressed. You must allow me to tell you how ardently I love and admire you.

ELIZABETH –

MR DARCY My feelings have been evoked to such a level that I cannot... They follow me and haunt me and I cannot commandeer control of them as I wish to. A desire to be near you, despite your inferiority and the circumstances of your family. A consumption of attraction that denies me rationality, indeed all sensibility as such. The obstacles of my standing will be arduous to negotiate, socially obviously, our match will be considered a most foolish degradation on my part. I am to be going against the wishes of my family, my friends, indeed my own judgement. The union can be considered nothing other than a form of wounding, of disabling myself. Yet I find I have no choice, when, it will only be pain, but, BUT, you must not deny me your hand.

MR DARCY *hold out his hand to* ELIZABETH. *She stares at it and at him. Lights go back to normal.* MISS DE BOURGH *wakes and smooths her hair.*

LADY CATHERINE I need a drink.

Curtain.

ACT TWO

Scene One: Darcy Writes

Sound effects polite applause. Lights up on **MODERN MB**, *she is wearing a headset and the TED talk logo is projected on the blackboard from earlier.*

MODERN MB I like to imagine Jane Austen, alive in the here and now. I like to imagine her reaction to our under-dressed pop singers, our kiss and tellers, morning-after-pill takers and porn stars. Poor, *confused,* Jane Austen who thought heroism was a well-kept secret and who rewarded virtue with marriage in all six of her novels – imagining her bafflement never fails to please me.

She reads from paper she is holding. She is quiet at first as if worried about being overheard.

ELIZABETH He must have scribbled this apology as soon as he arrived home. "I write without any intention of paining you, but I demand of it your justice. You have committed two offences of a very different nature…"

MODERN MB I do not blame Austen for being old fashioned, she could hardly help it. I cannot be angry with a writer whose idea of radical feminism was to send a female character on a long walk!

Sound effects polite laughter.

ELIZABETH *(filthy fury)* All offence has been *received* by me! His letter is written with the arrogance of Zeus himself, it is intended only to provoke, how did I DARE to reject him and so on. I won't read it.

MR DARCY *appears at the desk in the drawing room.*

MR DARCY How to outline my defence?

ELIZABETH *attempts to throw the paper away but it ends up back in front of her face.* MR DARCY *is scribbling and looking stressed. He reads a sentence from the paper in front of him.*

(*reading*) "I saw, in common with others that Mr Bingley preferred your eldest sister. At the Netherfield ball, it became clear that my friend's attentions had led to talk of potential marriage. I watched my friend and your sister closely, and while I witnessed huge partiality on his side, I could detect nothing but polite cheerfulness on hers..."

ELIZABETH She loves him! What would she do? What can she, what can any of us do but stand there and smile and wait and stand and—

MODERN MB A writer's work can be considered a response to their culture. What are they reacting to, what normality shaped them? Any biographical details can be relevant.

MR DARCY "her demeanour was cool, and..."

MR DARCY/ELIZABETH "...I judged her heart unlikely to be touched!"

ELIZABETH (*reading*) "...I lectured Mr Bingley as to the evils of such a choice. But this remonstrance had no bearing on his emotion towards your sister. It was only with my conviction that his affections were not returned by her, wherewith he agreed to return to London. And once there, never to return."

MODERN MB Would Austen's works have been so romantic, if she hadn't suffered her own disappointment? We know from her letters that she enjoyed a flirtation with one Tom LeFroy. A gentleman with whom she danced and argued wittily until his family intervened and sent him away.

ELIZABETH Oh, Poor Jane.

MODERN MB Without this experience, could she have written a character suffering the same circumstance? A character with her own name...

ELIZABETH Does he expect me to forgive him his interference because he cannot fathom affection or feelings or anything about the world?

MR DARCY And how to convey what happened with Wickham?

TED projection goes, light goes up on students sitting near blackboard. ELIZABETH *joins them.*

STUDENT LYDIA Why's she walking around the countryside crying? Why doesn't she—

STUDENT KITTY Why doesn't she tell everyone that Darcy proposed to her?

TEACHER ELIZABETH She is a private woman. She respects *his* privacy.

STUDENT KITTY She hates him! She basically told him that, and he kept Janet and Bingles apart.

STUDENT LYDIA Mr Binbags.

STUDENT KITTY He didn't tell Binbags that Janet was in London.

TEACHER ELIZABETH "Jane".

STUDENT KITTY And he made the fit one poor.

TEACHER ELIZABETH We're about to discover Wickham's secret...

STUDENT LYDIA He's a zombie.

STUDENT KITTY Yeah, where *are* the zombies?

MR DARCY *stands in front of the students and reads his letter while they comment.*

MR DARCY *(reading)* "As to my second defence, I hope it will not bring you too much pain. My excellent father..."

STUDENT KITTY Bragging...

MR DARCY "...died about five years ago. In his steady attachment to Mr Wickham, he left instructions that if he were to take holy orders..."

TEACHER ELIZABETH If Wickham became a Vicar...

STUDENT LYDIA Duh.

MR DARCY "...a valuable family living would be made for him. And a legacy for one thousand pounds."

STUDENT LYDIA What's that in today's money?

TEACHER ELIZABETH A lot. Tens of thousands.

STUDENT LYDIA And in Euros?

MR DARCY "Mr Wickham wrote shortly afterwards and told me he was resolved against taking orders..."

STUDENT LYDIA (smug) Becoming a Vicar.

MR DARCY "...and had decided to study the law. He asked if it would be unreasonable to request some immediate pecuniary."

STUDENT LYDIA Euros.

MR DARCY "I agreed to give him three thousand pounds. And heard nothing for around two years. And then a letter..."

STUDENT KITTY So many boring letters...

STUDENT LYDIA When will he fall in the lake and take his shirt off?

MR DARCY (reading) "He assured me his circumstances were exceedingly bad. He had now decided he *would* be ordained after all, if I could assist him with the living promised to him by my father."

STUDENT LYDIA But...?

STUDENT KITTY What a hustler.

MR DARCY "You will hardly blame me for refusing to comply."

Lights dim on **MR DARCY** *and school room.*

ELIZABETH *(voice over)* The same Mr Wickham? This must be falsehood.

Lights up on the film edit booth. **MODERN MARY** *and* **GRAHAM** *as before. They are staring at a monitor.*

GRAHAM I'm going to change the grade on that – there, more lilac. For her eyes.

MODERN MARY She could seem cold here? Self-hating.

GRAHAM I want to go closer in, further and further towards her face-in, in, in and suddenly...

GRAHAM *clicks something and sits back proudly.*

Flowers in a field.

MODERN MARY Are you joking?

GRAHAM And Darcy boy's voice over the top of it.

GRAHAM *clicks something.*

DARCY *(offstage)* "Now I am obliged to tell you the details that bring me most distress. I would not concern to tell another human being unless I must."

MODERN MARY No fields, let them hear the words.

GRAHAM If they wanted words they would've read the book.

DARCY *(offstage)* Last summer, my sister Georgiana was persuaded to believe herself in love.

GRAHAM What about Lizzy and Darcy kissing projected onto the paper of the letter? As if that is what she is thinking about?

MODERN MARY He's describing the seduction of his young sister. Stolen away to the seaside by Wickham so that he could marry her and get all her money – he's a shit, this is shit, Elizabeth *hates* men she is not fantasising about...

GRAHAM She does NOT hate men.

MODERN MARY The unfairness then. No flowers. Don't soften this. She must doubt it, and then *feel* it.

GRAHAM *stares at* **MODERN MARY**. *He grabs her face.*

GRAHAM I love you.

MODERN MARY Get off...

GRAHAM Kiss me.

MODERN MARY Stop it...

Blackout on film edit, lights up on school.

TEACHER ELIZABETH She was wrong about both men.

STUDENT LYDIA How is this her fault?

TEACHER ELIZABETH She liked the man who gave her attention and despised the man who didn't.

STUDENT KITTY Darcy was negging her.

STUDENT LYDIA When a guy ignores or criticises ya to make ya like him.

TEACHER ELIZABETH Duh.

Scene Two: Dinner At Longbourn

Energetic musical interlude as Longbourn and its inhabitants are created fully on stage and in appropriate dress.

The **BENNETS** *surround a table eating dinner.*

MRS BENNET Why is everyone so quiet and glum? We are all of us back together.

MR BENNET We are eating.

MRS BENNET It's a celebration.

MR BENNET Let us each concentrate on our—

LYDIA I AM SULKING IF YOU MUST KNOW.

MR BENNET ...plate.

MRS BENNET Tell us everything about London, Jane?

JANE *(solemn)* I am pleased to be back.

MR BENNET Don't look pleased.

JANE I am.

MR BENNET You look miserable.

ELIZABETH Papa...

MRS BENNET It was a wasted trip.

JANE I was very well taken care of, I attended the theatre.

KITTY OH I want to go to the theatre.

LYDIA *I* would rather – no! I'm not talking to any of you.

MR BENNET Why was it a wasted trip?

MRS BENNET Because Mr B—

ELIZABETH *(quickly)* Did I tell you all about Mrs Collin's affinity with poultry?

KITTY Charlotte?

MARY Chickens?

MRS BENNET Does she trick her way into their hencoop, does she? Does she pretend to be all simpering and then steal the rooster and keep all the eggs for herself? And now all the other hens must leave the coop?

MARY Does she sleep with the hens?

ELIZABETH Mrs Collins is making our cousin very happy and seems most assured a wife.

JANE I feel for her.

ELIZABETH *(to* JANE*)* You should write – she is lonely. She is talking to the chickens!

MR BENNET More sensible than my cousin.

MRS BENNET I suppose she asks after your father's health?

ELIZABETH She is fond of father.

MRS BENNET She awaits his death with open arms!

JANE Mother...

ELIZABETH Really...

MR BENNET I am quite looking forward to it myself.

MRS BENNET Oh yes, let's all have a joke about it!

LYDIA *(to* MR BENNET*)* When you are dead I can go to Brighton.

KITTY Can you die of gout?

MRS BENNET That entailment law should be illegal!

(to LYDIA*)* You'll be in the workhouse.

> MR BENNET *slaps the table very hard. It is tense. Then* KITTY *remembers.*

KITTY Oh!

LYDIA What?

KITTY Did we tell them about Wickham?

MRS BENNET Oh yes did we tell them?

ELIZABETH *(concerned)* What have you learned of him?

LYDIA He is set to marry Miss King.

ELIZABETH Oh...

MRS BENNET You missed your chance there Lizzy.

KITTY He fell in love with her the moment she inherited eight thousand.

MARY I don't think I *could* live in a hen house.

JANE I am happy for Miss King.

MRS BENNET *(to JANE)* Are you pining away my dear? Are you dying of a broken heart? Eat your cabbage.

LYDIA He won't go through with it.

MRS BENNET She's got those horrible freckles.

ELIZABETH She's got eight thousand pounds.

MR BENNET *(fury)* CAN WE HAVE ONE MEAL WITHOUT A CONSTANT TALK OF MONEY AND POUNDS AND CASH AND INHERITANCE AND—

MRS BENNET If you had been a better man and provided one...

MR BENNET *slaps table again.* JANE *silently cries.* ELIZABETH *holds her hand.*

MR BENNET Now we change the subject.

LYDIA Sir? My father, I implore you. PLEASE may I go to Brighton?

KITTY And I?

LYDIA *(to KITTY, nicely)* You were not invited.

MR BENNET I will not give you money.

LYDIA I would be the guest of Mr and Mrs Forster.

MRS BENNET She will need new dresses.

MR BENNET NO.

LYDIA But I may go?

KITTY And I?

MR BENNET You may. But only that there might be one less idiotic woman at my dinner table and that you may learn the hard lesson that as a female with no income it does not matter how pretty a bonnet you are wearing.

ELIZABETH Father, she should not—

MRS BENNET Hooray for your father!

ELIZABETH My sisters should not be behaving in this way, chasing soldiers around the country...

LYDIA YAY!!

> **LYDIA** *gets up and starts dancing around the table,* **MRS BENNET** *is conducting her.*

KITTY *(weeping)* Please may I be invited?

ELIZABETH *(to* **MR BENNET***)* The behaviour of my sisters reflects on all of us.

MR BENNET *(sarcastic)* Oh yes, driving away your suitors, are they? All queuing up around the neighbourhood...

LYDIA Absolutely everybody is jealous of me!

KITTY This is most cruel and unfair!

MR BENNET Have my plate sent to my study. I will eat in there. I am sick.

MRS BENNET *(to* **JANE***)* You should die of a broken heart, that'll teach him.

> *As* **MR BENNET** *exits, everyone else moves.*

KITTY It is MY HEART that is broken!

LYDIA My heart is positively bursting!

LYDIA *exits followed by* MRS BENNET *and* KITTY. JANE *and* ELIZABETH *stand together.* MARY *sits at the table alone.*

MARY I've no idea what I'd even say to the other chickens.

ELIZABETH *hugs* JANE *on the other side of the room.*

JANE I used to be better at holding it all in.

ELIZABETH It is a lot, to go from the peace of our Aunt and Uncle's, back to...our family.

JANE I'll never get an answer, will I? Why didn't he come? I suppose that *is* my answer.

ELIZABETH You may still – there could be an explanation.

JANE I'll learn again, how to swallow. And then forget.

ELIZABETH You must ignore Mother...

JANE And her sensible advice to die as revenge?

ELIZABETH *laughs. Lights and TED projection on* MODERN MB.

Scene Three: TED And Rehearsals

MODERN MB After he was sent away, Jane Austen never met Tom LeFroy again. He married happily and had several children, while the author herself remained unwed until... well until she died, spoiler alert!

Sound effects polite laughter. Lights brighten for modern rehearsal state. A radio is playing music. **MODERN MB** *picks up a clipboard, moves a couple of chairs.* **MODERN WICKHAM** *enters glugging from a bottle of water, he turns the radio down as he passes it.*

MODERN WICKHAM Don't come near me, I'm hanging – I stink!

MODERN MB I thought we could do some character work before the others get here. Some hot-seating perhaps, get under his skin and—

WICKHAM *sits the wrong way around on a chair.* **MODERN ELIZABETH** *enters.*

MODERN WICKHAM I've got a lot of problems with the script to be honest.

MODERN MB *(to* **MODERN ELIZABETH***)* What are you doing here?

MODERN ELIZABETH *(eyes on* **WICKHAM***)* I had a casting in town. I didn't want to wait outside.

MODERN MB We're working.

MODERN WICKHAM What was it for?

MODERN ELIZABETH *(shrugs)* Only a play.

MODERN WICKHAM *visibly loses interest and turns back to* **MODERN MB.**

MODERN WICKHAM I think the problems I'm having with my character—

MODERN ELIZABETH You're doing *so* well.

MODERN WICKHAM ...are because the script, well I think everyone is really judging him especially the writer. And so, he is not very sympathetic.

MODERN MB Is he supposed to be?

MODERN WICKHAM He's the hero.

> **MODERN ELIZABETH** *and* **MODERN MB** *look at each other.*

Yeah, like at the moment everyone is judging him for going off with the Darcy girl—

MODERN MB You think there was love there?

MODERN WICKHAM I just think what if that girl was really horny, and she was the one instigating everything?

MODERN MB I see.

MODERN ELIZABETH That's a really good point, are we denying female agency?

MODERN MB No. We are relying on a novel, which tells us Georgiana Darcy is a timid, shy young woman.

MODERN WICKHAM Maybe Jane Austen was leaving stuff out of the book? Because it would have been too racy? Maybe Georgiana in real life was like, a real up-for-it tease, like some quiet girls are?

MODERN MB For God's sake, we are debating a fictional character, or rather you are re-writing her...

MODERN WICKHAM Yes, I'd like to re-write my bits please.

MODERN ELIZABETH Maybe Wickham and Elizabeth could have a *proper* moment?

MODERN WICKHAM *(shakes head)* Not that.

MODERN ELIZABETH Or maybe...

MODERN WICKHAM I want everyone to see how brave it was for Wickham to be poor in the olden days.

MODERN MB Let's try and capture that within the existing lines. There is a moment between Lizzy and Mr Wickham, before he leaves for Merryton – if you want to show his depths then...

MODERN ELIZABETH *(keen)* Page?

MODERN WICKHAM *finds page on script and reads as lights change. A garden is created. Their scripts are left on rehearsal chairs.*

Scene Four: Wickham And Elizabeth

MR WICKHAM Shall we take a walk in the garden before we lose the last of this beautiful day?

ELIZABETH I should stay.

MR WICKHAM Since when has my audacious friend worried about "should"?

ELIZABETH Congratulations on your engagement.

MR WICKHAM Ah.

ELIZABETH Sincerely.

MR WICKHAM Miss King she is—

ELIZABETH I hope you will do well by her. She is a sweet woman.

MR WICKHAM She is a *distant* woman.

ELIZABETH A wife should have self-control.

MR WICKHAM Birmingham. A persuasive Uncle showed his hand.

ELIZABETH Well...

MR WICKHAM And wallet. Whisked her away from me!

ELIZABETH I hope she's—

MR WICKHAM Story of my life!

ELIZABETH —

MR WICKHAM I missed you while you were gone. And now the regiment are off to Brighton it will be your turn to miss me!

ELIZABETH I am away myself. To Derbyshire with my Aunt and Uncle.

MR WICKHAM Will you write to your Wickham?

ELIZABETH I was very impressed with Rosings, Lady Catherine De Bourgh...

MR WICKHAM As is intended.

ELIZABETH ...and her visitors.

MR WICKHAM Yes?

ELIZABETH I have grown to know our acquaintance far better.

MR WICKHAM She's so incredibly self-confident. She once gave me detailed instruction on how to shave my own face, a subject she can have no familiarity with.

ELIZABETH Not Lady Catherine.

MR WICKHAM *(laughing)* ...judging from her chin.

ELIZABETH I saw Mr Darcy every day for almost three weeks.

MR WICKHAM How unbearable – that his pomposity should swell up and interrupt your trip.

ELIZABETH Quite the opposite, his behaviour was most civil.

MR WICKHAM Perhaps he has hit his head? Or taken to opium?

ELIZABETH His ways were in no way changed. Rather it is I who has begun to see him rather differently.

MR WICKHAM *(I hate this)* I am so glad to hear of this.

MR WICKHAM bows to ELIZABETH and turns to leave her, walking straight into KITTY.

I must be off little one, give my regards to your par—

KITTY TAKE ME TO BRIGHTON!

KITTY sobs and wraps her whole body around MR WICKHAM. She could also pass him a script somehow.

Make them take me! You take me!

ELIZABETH *(to MR WICKHAM, pointed)* Our respectable friend? Taking young women to the seaside?

Lights change back to rehearsal scene. MODERN WICKHAM throws script to the floor.

MODERN WICKHAM How dare she judge him? She who should have married her cousin and considered herself lucky. This whole play is just some unmarried virgin's romance fantasy.

Scene Five: Gardiners

Sound effects piano music begins, lights change, become late evening. **ELIZABETH** *sits at a piano with* **JANE.**

JANE They'll be here soon.

ELIZABETH I can't wait!

JANE But you're leaving me!

ELIZABETH I need to walk and walk until my mind is quiet.

JANE What are you always thinking about lately?

ELIZABETH I am *so* confused about men Jane.

JANE They're not like in books, are they?

Sound effects bell rings.

Kiss every peak for me, stroke every lake.

ELIZABETH I'll write every view to the best of my ability, that you may see them too.

MRS BENNET *can be heard offstage with greetings and exaltations and then as she enters:*

MRS BENNET ...oh, that's a shame. LIZZY, MY BROTHER'S HERE!

MR *and* **MRS GARDINER** *enter followed by* **MARY** *and* **KITTY.**

MR GARDINER ...it's just business. Can't be helped.

ELIZABETH Are we not going?

MRS GARDINER Good afternoon Ladies.

MRS GARDINER *greets* **JANE** *and* **ELIZABETH** *warmly.*

MR GARDINER Our Northern adventure has been cut short I'm afraid...

ELIZABETH Oh.

MRS GARDINER A whistle-stop week in Derbyshire my lamb.

MR GARDINER I have some documents to collect that way so it all works out well.

ELIZABETH No lakes at all?

MRS BENNET Don't be ungrateful Lizzy – you are lucky to be taken anywhere.

KITTY *(sulking)* You *are* lucky.

MARY *(knowing)* I suppose you'll be wanting to sketch?

MRS GARDINER Shortened or not, let's not waste a moment of our holiday!

KITTY Will there be soldiers?

MRS GARDINER I'm sure we'll not meet a soul!

MR GARDINER We are looking for kingfishers and deer, not people!

> **ELIZABETH** *is picking up her suitcase and kissing her sisters goodbye.* **MARY** *passes her something.*

MARY *(whispers)* You may take my pencil, but beware, it is very, *very* good at shading.

MR GARDINER Although we may pop into Pemberley House as the grounds are so scenic.

MRS GARDINER Yes, that is top of my must-see list!

> **ELIZABETH** *is being swept towards the door.*

ELIZABETH Pemberley?

MRS BENNET Goodbye then!

Scene Six: Back To School

*Sound effects door slam. Lighting change to school room.
Blackboard obscures the stage.* STUDENT KITTY *is at a
desk.* MODERN ELIZABETH *enters.*

TEACHER ELIZABETH You should be enjoying lunch, what are
you hiding in here from?

STUDENT KITTY I'M ANNOYED! I need to speak to you miss!

MODERN ELIZABETH 'Sup? Sorry.

STUDENT KITTY I did the reading, and she is going away –
Lizzy, she is going exactly to where Mr Darcy lives – why
would she go in?

MODERN ELIZABETH Well she has to, for the story, she has to
speak to the Housekeeper.

MODERN KITTY That's annoying too – how can you "love"
someone you call "master"?

MODERN ELIZABETH Now that could be an interesting essay?

MODERN KITTY My essay is, "How frustrating is this book?"

MODERN ELIZABETH Lizzy is assured that Darcy is not at
Pemberley and will not be home for several days, she does
check, but she can't say *why* she would want to avoid him
without—

MODERN KITTY It's too obvious, it's embarrassing – making
best friends with his servants and looking at tiny pictures
of him and getting wet about how nice his house is.

MODERN ELIZABETH Excuse me...

*Pemberly builds under next few lines. Dialogue gets
quieter.*

MODERN KITTY Was this really the olden days? Did women
get a hard-on for property?

MODERN ELIZABETH There is so much to unpack in that sentence...

MODERN KITTY I don't think I can read anymore, I'm cringing.

Scene Seven: Pemberley

HOUSEKEEPER, MR *and* MRS GARDINER *are walking through a rose garden with a beautiful house in the distance behind them.*

HOUSEKEEPER It can still take my breath away. I remind myself to really see it, not to take it for granted.

MRS GARDINER You've been ever so kind to show us around like this.

HOUSEKEEPER A pleasure for me also...

ELIZABETH *enters walking a few steps behind them. She is deep in thought.*

MR GARDINER Like working in a museum or a gallery or—

Sound effects horseshoes and wheels on gravel.

HOUSEKEEPER My heart, what lucky circumstance!

ELIZABETH *stops completely still looking offstage.*

You are in for the most timely of treats, my master is early!

MR DARCY *(offstage)* Who's this? Visitors!

HOUSEKEEPER May I introduce the Gardiners sir, admiring your grounds.

MR DARCY *enters, he is noticibly more cheerful than when we have met him previously.* ELIZABETH *is directly behind her relatives.*

MR DARCY And a wonderful day for it! I've rushed back from – who cares, I'm here. Welcome to Pemb—

MR DARCY *sees* ELIZABETH. *They stare at each other. She wants to die.*

ELIZABETH Good afternoon, Sir.

MR DARCY Good afternoon.

HOUSEKEEPER Miss says you have acquaintance?

MR DARCY Indeed we—

ELIZABETH Met at a ball once...

MR DARCY ...are friends.

ELIZABETH Allow me to introduce my Aunt and Uncle, my relatives from London.

There is shaking of hands and smart bowing. With murmurs of pleasure and politeness. **HOUSEKEEPER** *looks between* **MR DARCY** *and* **ELIZABETH** *and then exits.*

MR DARCY I hope you will allow me to continue your tour myself.

ELIZABETH We do not wish to intrude.

MR DARCY Nonsense, I am awarded no greater pleasure than seeing the most beautiful place in the world through fresh eyes.

MRS GARDINER You are most kind.

MR DARCY Can I show you the river, does Sir fish?

MR GARDINER Nothing I like better.

MR DARCY You must come back tomorrow early and catch a trout, they are huge this season.

MR GARDINER You have excited me mightily.

MRS GARDINER *(whisper to* **ELIZABETH***)* He is absolutely nothing as you described.

ELIZABETH *(to* DARCY*)* We do not wish to put you out.

MR DARCY I have always wanted to show you.

ELIZABETH falls quiet and is embarrassed. **MR DARCY** *turns and begins to walk, the others follow.*

MRS GARDINER Well isn't this lovely?

MR DARCY It really is! OH!

MR DARCY *stops and turns back to look at* **ELIZABETH.**

Will you dine with us tomorrow, when my sister arrives?

ELIZABETH *is dumbfounded.*

All of you? It would be the loveliest—

MRS GARDINER We would love to. We are at the Inn on the Crosskey Street, here for two more days.

MR DARCY Such good fortune, this timing!

MR DARCY *strides away,* **MR GARDINER** *keeps pace with him and they exit.* **MRS GARDINER** *takes* **ELIZABETH***'s arm as they follow.*

MRS GARDINER You are a very secretive young woman.

Scene Eight: Letter To Lizzy

Film edit set up. It seems there is no one there. Still on screens of ELIZABETH's *face looking horrified as* MR DARCY *arrived in previous scene. There are some mumbling noises, then* MODERN MARY *and* GRAHAM *emerge from underneath the desk. They sit back on their chairs. She looks at him, shakes her head and laughs. He lifts her hand and kisses it.*

GRAHAM I do love you.

MODERN MARY You don't.

GRAHAM It's just a new kind of love. One neither of us recognise.

MODERN MARY *leans forward and kisses him. It is tender and sweet. Behind them, a small sitting room builds.* ELIZABETH *and* MISS DARCY *sit facing each other.*

MISS DARCY I so enjoyed meeting you yesterday. I hope you do not mind my immediately rushing over.

ELIZABETH Don't be silly.

MISS DARCY I am silly, I'm so keen for a friend!

ELIZABETH We are friends. Can you stay for tea?

MISS DARCY I would love nothing more! My brother has talked of you so fondly, and it is all true!

ELIZABETH I get so shy with compliments.

MISS DARCY Nonsense, you are the most confident woman I have ever met!

ELIZABETH I am strident, I must learn to stop my tongue, but my thoughts run and then...

MISS DARCY I find you most inspiring!

SERVANT *enters.*

ELIZABETH May we have some tea?

SERVANT Of course madam. And you've post.

SERVANT *passes envelopes and exits.* **ELIZABETH** *doesn't look at them at first.*

ELIZABETH Confidence, truly trusting in oneself, I don't know how one achieves that really.

MISS DARCY At least you do not tremble to sing or play in front of people.

ELIZABETH That is merely not caring that I am bad.

MISS DARCY Not true! You are marvellous!

ELIZABETH Or perhaps as I have a large and noisy family, no one was ever focusing on me for very long – I am invisible in a crowd. Or I feel that way, it can be freeing.

MISS DARCY I hope I shall meet your sister Jane.

ELIZABETH Oh I hope it, she is an angel, you wouldn't bel—

ELIZABETH *notices the letters in her hand.*

How funny! I am seeing her handwriting in front of me!

ELIZABETH *passes an envelope to* **MISS DARCY.**

Look how neat that script is? Only a divine heart could write that neatly!

MISS DARCY I am positively jealous!

ELIZABETH I write like a gorilla.

ELIZABETH *takes the letter back, she is holding two identical envelopes.*

But why has she written to me twice?

MISS DARCY I wish I had sisters.

ELIZABETH Can I be awfully rude?

MISS DARCY Please!

ELIZABETH *rips and reads first one letter and then the other. She is very tense.* SERVANT *returns with tea and* MISS DARCY *pours and stirs in little movements, and sits back elegantly to drink.*

ELIZABETH I am so dreadfully sorry. I can't... I will have to see you back to your carriage.

MISS DARCY Is something wrong? With your sister?

ELIZABETH It is something, oh... I am so sorry.

ELIZABETH *begins to cry,* MISS DARCY *stands, she is helpless. She takes* ELIZABETH*'s hand. Lights change, dim.* MISS DARCY *exits.* ELIZABETH *is in same position. There is a knock at the door.*

Aunty?

MR DARCY *(offstage)* May I come in?

ELIZABETH Oh.

ELIZABETH *stands up.* MR DARCY *enters.*

MR DARCY Please forgive me. My sister was beside herself with worry and... And... We could not bear to be so near and offer no assistance so... Can I help you? Do you need to get back home? I could—

ELIZABETH Oh, yes but... I don't know what can be done and, it is too too terrible. I keep thinking, how to fix the... What she's done and...she has ruined all of us. It is done.

MR DARCY Your mother?

ELIZABETH *passes the open letters to* MR DARCY *who begins to read.*

ELIZABETH Not her, my poor mother.

MR DARCY He has struck again.

ELIZABETH She is a baby, a ridiculous baby.

MR DARCY But why was she at Brighton without chaperone?

ELIZABETH She snuck out in the night, keep reading, she did have chaperone, but they did not realise how close she had become to Wickham.

MR DARCY He is a, a snake who escapes notice.

ELIZABETH But she has nothing. He will not marry her for—

MR DARCY Where are they now?

ELIZABETH She says up to Scotland, but nobody knows.

MR DARCY I shall get you home. I will arrange it.

ELIZABETH I'll leave a note for my Aunt – you'll not tell anyone, please, if we could keep this quiet.

MR DARCY I'll not tell a soul.

ELIZABETH ...and your sister...

MR DARCY ...especially. I'll not have her hurt by him increase.

ELIZABETH I suppose people will know eventually.

Scene Nine: Lydia's Return

ELIZABETH *begins to weep.* MR DARCY *turns and exits the room.* ELIZABETH *looks after him but says nothing. She stays where she is as the scene changes, the* BENNET*'s drawing room and inhabitants assemble around her as she suffers, only* MR BENNET *is absent, the mood is sombre.* MRS BENNET *waits at a window.*

MARY What was it we used to do?

Nobody looks or MARY *or answers. She looks down at her hands.*

How does one know if one is a ghost?

ELIZABETH Father is with Uncle?

Silence. Moments pass.

MARY *(to* ELIZABETH*)* Perhaps you are dead also. Can you see me?

ELIZABETH Yes Mary.

MARY Shall we try the wall?

ELIZABETH Has there been *any* post today?

JANE Nothing.

ELIZABETH Perhaps this evening?

JANE Maybe...

KITTY Poor Lydia.

ELIZABETH *(whisper to* JANE*)* This is my fault. If I had told of Wickham's previous behaviour...

MRS BENNET *(suddenly crazed)* They must make him marry her, he must, they must be found and marched to the nearest church and if your father lets me down this time, if he lets me down again, why oh why did he let her go, such a permissive man, too trusting, he has brought ruin to us

all. I will drown myself, I will tie myself to – what, a chair?
Give me your chair Kitty...

Sound effects horse and carriage on gravel. **KITTY** *stands and passes her chair to her mother and sees.*

KITTY SOMEONE IS HERE! PAPA!

MARY *goes over to the wall and tries to push her hand against it...*

MRS BENNET MY HUSBAND! Why have they retu—

MRS BENNET *faints onto the floor, the chair she is holding crashes.* **JANE, KITTY** *and* **ELIZABETH** *rush to help her. They attempt to lift her.*

MARY *(to* **ELIZABETH***)* Mother has died to join us?

MR BENNET *enters.* **MRS BENNET** *struggles against her daughters holding her in the air.*

MRS BENNET Where is she? My baby girl, my—

LYDIA *and* **MR WICKHAM** *enter arm in arm.*

LYDIA *(stately)* I am here Mama. Nobody's baby any longer.
You may call me Mrs Wickham!

LYDIA *laughs and rushes to display her ring.*
MRS BENNET *screeches and kisses* **MR WICKHAM.**

MRS BENNET Congratulations you beautiful, beautiful – OH!
I knew you would – how romantic!

MRS BENNET *and* **LYDIA** *jump excitedly around while everyone else seems very morose.*

MR BENNET It was quicker to return than to write.

LYDIA I'm married! I'm the youngest and the first and—

MR WICKHAM *(to* **ELIZABETH***)* You may call me brother.

ELIZABETH Congratulations Mr Wickham.

LYDIA Mother are you proud of me?

MRS BENNET So proud, my darling.

KITTY Will he be in our... Where will you sleep... With?

MR BENNET They are not to stay long.

LYDIA We have a cottage, everything has been sorted for us!

MR BENNET We will be indebted to your Uncle for a long time hence.

LYDIA I'm so excited!

KITTY *(to* **LYDIA***)* Have you...?

LYDIA You may consider me a *woman*.

MR BENNET *(to* **MRS BENNET***)* We arranged a situation in Shropshire.

MR WICKHAM I will finally do the work of God.

MRS BENNET That is too far!

MR BENNET I think under the circumstances...

LYDIA How jealous my sisters are!

MRS BENNET You'll stay with us awhile yet?

MR WICKHAM I'm afraid...

MR BENNET There are conditions. The newly weds will be off tonight.

LYDIA Kitty help me pack!

MRS BENNET What unfairness, you should have dresses, you should have *things* to take.

  MRS BENNET *rushes offstage.*

LYDIA Who needs *anything* when one is in love?

  LYDIA *brazenly kisses* **WICKHAM**. **JANE, ELIZABETH** *and* **KITTY** *look so sad.* **MR BENNET** *reaches out for* **MARY**.

As he touches her, she looks at their joined hands, and then him happily.

MARY I'm alive!

MR BENNET You'll none of you go anywhere, ever. So don't ask. And I'll not hear anything else about a soldier at anytime, if I am eating or – ever.

TED talk state created, BENNETS *stay onstage,* LYDIA *and* WICKHAM *exit.* MODERN MB *enters.*

MODERN MB A modern reader must remind herself that while Austen's characters seem familiar to us, their reality isn't. A woman in Regency England had the legal status of a child. Unwed women remained the property of their father, while any that married would find belongings, money and physical autonomy passed into her husband's ownership. He would vote on her behalf, control the household and could not be denied conjugal rights. The question I ask is, and I ask it often...how could what we call "love" exist in such circumstances?

Scene Ten: Bingley Proposes

Lights brighten in Longbourn drawing room as MODERN
MB *exits.* KITTY *and* MARY *are playing some kind of
board game.* JANE *and* ELIZABETH *are reading books.*
MR BENNET *is doing a crossword.*

MARY Shall I play us something?

MR BENNET No.

ELIZABETH Has she written?

MR BENNET She'll be too busy now.

KITTY Doing *what* father?

> ELIZABETH, JANE, MARY *and* KITTY *all look expectantly
> at* MR BENNET.

MR BENNET *(sex)* Cleaning.

> MRS BENNET *enters.*

MRS BENNET *(sex)* Horrid old cleaning.

KITTY Can't she get a woman to do it for her?

MR BENNET I'm sure she will, in time.

> MRS BENNET *laughs, then remembers.*

MRS BENNET Cook says a party has arrived at Netherfield.

MR BENNET I thought he was selling.

MRS BENNET Perhaps he has.

KITTY Were there soldiers?

MRS BENNET You know I don't like to gossip.

> *Beat and reactions off this.*

> *(to* JANE*)* He could be back...

ELIZABETH *(firm)* Whomever is in that house is of no interest to this one.

MR BENNET Well said Lizzy.

JANE *goes to look from the window.*

MRS BENNET I'll send someone over to welcome them to the district...

KITTY As long as that old goat isn't back.

MRS BENNET ...then we'll know.

MRS BENNET *exits.*

MARY A goat?

KITTY Poking his nose in where it isn't needed.

MARY It's called butting. They can't help it.

ELIZABETH Who?

KITTY Darcy the B—

MARY Goats.

ELIZABETH *takes* KITTY *away to the side and whispers.*

ELIZABETH What of Mr Darcy?

KITTY I hate him.

ELIZABETH Why should you hate him?

KITTY It's HIS fault about Lydia. He chased them to London and forced them to church and promised Wickham thousands and thousands if he would up and leave to Shropshire and be a vicar and—

MARY *(shouting over)* It's because they don't have hands.

ELIZABETH How do you know this?

JANE *approaches them.*

KITTY Lydia made me swear on my life that no one should know.

    MRS BENNET *enters and runs to the window.*

MRS BENNET SOMEONE IS COMING OVER!

MR BENNET I'm to my study. If it is George the Third himself – let me be.

    MR BENNET *exits.*

ELIZABETH *(to* **KITTY***)* You should never tell secrets when you've been trusted.

JANE *(to* **ELIZABETH***)* Why was he there?

ELIZABETH I cannot think.

    MRS BENNET *runs from the room while shouting.*

MRS BENNET THERE COMES A MAN ON A HORSE.

MARY *(to no one)* They only have their face. They can't help that.

    JANE *looks from the window.*

JANE It is him.

ELIZABETH Mr Bingley?

    JANE *goes to a chair and picks up her book and pretends to read.* **ELIZABETH** *runs to pick up a book also. They sit awkwardly, seem posed.* **KITTY** *rushes to join them but has no book so looks at her hands instead.*

KITTY I knew I should have learned to read.

    MRS BENNET *bursts in with* **MR BINGLEY** *who takes off his hat and seems out of breath.*

MR BINGLEY Good afternoon.

    JANE, ELIZABETH *and* **KITTY** *all nod demurely.*

MARY We were just talking about goats.

MRS BENNET Mary, could I see you upstairs?

MARY *exits.* MRS BENNET *does crazy head movements until* KITTY *jumps up and follows.*

KITTY I wish to go upstairs also...

JANE *and* BINGLEY *smile at each other.* ELIZABETH *stares at her book as if reading.*

JANE Have you recently returned from London?

MR BINGLEY *(grinning)* Yes.

KITTY *barges back in. She stands behind* MR BINGLEY *and makes frantic head gestures for* ELIZABETH *to leave. After some pointed ignoring, as* MR BINGLEY *turns around and notices.*

KITTY Mother says you've to do that thing now, like you promised, with the, fabrics.

ELIZABETH Please excuse me.

ELIZABETH *and* KITTY *exit.* MR BINGLEY *instantly stands.*

MR BINGLEY *(composed)* Miss Bennet... Jane, may I call you Jane?

JANE Yes.

MR BINGLEY I love you so much I feel sick.

Sound effects loud applause. MR BINGLEY *and* JANE *should stay on stage, there should be a one-kneed proposal and some affectionate touching. The TED state is created also.*

MODERN MB The answer, the only answer I have – is that "love" exists in all and every state. It survives throughout unfairness and atrocity. Love as a base, animal attraction and attachment lives even when only in our imagination. As I surmise was the case with Austen herself. While her poverty denied her the man she loved, she created another universe, where an equally fortuneless, fictional Jane got a better ending.

Blackout on TED state.

JANE *(cries)* Yes, oh Charles, yes...I'm so happy.

> JANE *and* MR BINGLEY *embrace for a few moments before* ELIZABETH *and* KITTY *fall into the room,* KITTY *runs to the piano and begins to bash out "RULE BRITANNIA".* MR BENNET *enters and there is much screaming and kissing and hugging.*

(to ELIZABETH*)* He didn't know I was in London.

ELIZABETH No one told him.

JANE He thought I had no feelings.

ELIZABETH But now he can be certain.

JANE I could surely explode or melt I, I wish you could feel happiness like this.

ELIZABETH My sister this is the happiest moment of my life!

> *Lights change and edit scene is created.* MODERN MARY *enters in cocktail dress and heels. Hair is different etc.*

GRAHAM Shit you look incredible.

MODERN MARY Well we won't win...

GRAHAM We deserve to.

MODERN MARY ...so might as well look good for the "disappointed face" shot.

GRAHAM It's insane. That dress is insane. You should always dress like this.

MODERN MARY We wouldn't get anything done.

> *Beat.*

You coming in the cab with me?

GRAHAM Ah, I can't.

MODERN MARY You gonna make me ask?

GRAHAM I dunno, what?

MODERN MARY Is your wife coming?

GRAHAM Er, sure.

> **MODERN MARY** *starts angrily packing a few things up into a bag.*

Don't hate me babe, it's our big night.

MODERN MARY It's not you I hate, Graham. It's myself.

> **MODERN MARY** *exits.*

Scene Eleven: Another Proposal

Lights change, back to Longbourn. ELIZABETH *is alone trying to concentrate on a book, she throws it.*

ELIZABETH It is not realistic.

ELIZABETH *retrieves the book and finds her page again.*

Am I supposed to swoon at this?

ELIZABETH *stares into space.*

Perhaps I am not a good *woman?* Maybe if I wrote poetry, tried to find beauty in grasses and ponies and—

There is a knock and a SERVANT *shows in* LADY CATHERINE DE BOURGH *and* MR COLLINS.

LADY CATHERINE I have sent your relatives into the garden.

ELIZABETH Good afternoon Lady Catherine.

LADY CATHERINE You will have been expecting me.

ELIZABETH Did you write? If so nothing has arr—

LADY CATHERINE You thought I would not intervene?

MR COLLINS Why must you ruin everything?

LADY CATHERINE You were entertained in my home. I gave generous advice on how to pack your suitcase and—

MR COLLINS I packed *so* neatly for this trip.

LADY CATHERINE I will not let you marry him.

ELIZABETH It is my sister who is to marry, though what business it is of yours—

MR COLLINS SHE WILL NOT MARRY!

LADY CATHERINE Not one of your wretched brethren will be marrying into my family.

ELIZABETH *Your* family? Is Mr Bingley...?

LADY CATHERINE Do not dissemble, outrageous creature. And has Darcy not proposed?

ELIZABETH I...I will refuse to answer that.

LADY CATHERINE I am a very, very powerful woman.

ELIZABETH You possess no power which entitles you to the contents of another's mind.

MR COLLINS SHOW HER YOUR MIND THIS INSTANT!

LADY CATHERINE You will refuse him.

ELIZABETH You will excuse me...

> **MR BENNET** *enters.*

MR BENNET Why do my daughters believe themselves banished from my house?

LADY CATHERINE I am leaving.

MR COLLINS *(to* **MR BENNET***)* The house remains theirs while you are standing.

> **LADY CATHERINE** *barges out.* **MR COLLINS** *looks around meaningfully and follows. Sound effects carriage several moments later.*

MR BENNET You won't believe the gossip – I can hardly stop laughing!

> **KITTY, MARY** *and* **JANE** *enter.*

KITTY Are you engaged Lizzy?

MR BENNET Of course she isn't.

JANE What did the Lady want?

ELIZABETH She was mistaken. Her information was long out of date.

KITTY As if you would want that horrid, haughty nephew of hers.

ELIZABETH He is a... It is not relevant. I'm going for a walk.

Outdoor state is created, **ELIZABETH** *is walking and suddenly* **MR DARCY** *is revealed. They stare at each other. He speaks stiltingly at first.*

MR DARCY I was, I am coming to see you. I am glad you are out. My aunt, this will sound very strange, but my Aunt has travelled to your house hoping to—

ELIZABETH She and I have spoken.

MR DARCY I am truly sorry.

ELIZABETH I am glad to see you.

MR DARCY Hello.

ELIZABETH I recently have become aware of the great service you have undertaken towards my family.

MR DARCY Your Uncle promised—

ELIZABETH Lydia told. I don't think I will ever be able to stop telling you how grateful I am for what you have done for us.

MR DARCY I did not do it for your them. I did it for you.

ELIZABETH I am undeserving of such friendship.

MR DARCY When we spoke once before—

ELIZABETH And you brought Bingley back!

MR DARCY I admitted to him at the first opportunity, that I was incorrect in my assessment of your sister's feeling.

ELIZABETH They will be so happy.

MR DARCY He brought himself back, without so much as stopping for lunch - he near killed the horses.

ELIZABETH I can't stop smiling.

MR DARCY I have to ask you, if...if your own feelings remain those expressed when last time we spoke, when I—

Moment, looking at each other. Close but not touching. It is too much.

ELIZABETH Do you want to walk?

MR DARCY Do you want to marry me?

ELIZABETH *laughs a bit.*

ELIZABETH Your aunt will have me killed.

MR DARCY I have the resources to protect you.

ELIZABETH You know it's just for Pemberley.

MR DARCY Obviously, what else have I to offer?

ELIZABETH I love you.

ELIZABETH *covers her face like she can't believe she said it.*

MR DARCY So you will?

ELIZABETH *nods.* **MR DARCY** *very slowly approaches to touch her, he can't believe he is allowed. She holds out a hand, he strokes it finger by finger, lifts it to his lips.*

ELIZABETH You have done so much for me already.

MR DARCY I love you.

ELIZABETH Can I ask for one more thing?

MR DARCY I wish so much to make you happy.

ELIZABETH May I break the news to Miss Bingley?

MR DARCY *lunges as if to kiss* **ELIZABETH** *but loses confidence and stops a few inches away. As he begins to back away,* **ELIZABETH** *puts her hands to his face and presses her lips on his.*

The End

A NOTE ABOUT PROPS AND LIGHTING

Please be free and creative when staging your production, you may choose to be more historically accurate than I have been or even less so. In my mind, if you are on a small budget everything can be done with a few brooms wearing coats and an old table (and some actors obviously). Lighting states to differentiate time and place will aid story telling greatly and I have indicated the most vital of these in stage directions. The original production had music composed by Emmy the Great, those songs and the score can be requested from her management and used alongside this text.

For further details please contact: Alun Llwyd

alun@turnstilemusic.net

Lightning Source UK Ltd.
Milton Keynes UK
UKOW01f0334140917
309144UK00005B/359/P